'… *musical stories to guide us through our emotional lives.*'
BAZ LUHRMANN

'*I would like to issue a caution: Mr Lawrence is peddling a
dangerous substance here. If you take too much of this
Swoon you could become a swoon loon – staggering down the
street, a head full of swoon tunes.*'
RICHARD TOGNETTI

'*I am afraid there are moments in life when even Schubert
has nothing to say to us. We must admit,
however, that they are our worst.*' *So says Madame Merle
from Henry James' Portrait of a Lady. Christopher Lawrence
gives readers and listeners more chance to respond to
the intrigue – this perfection of harmony of voice
and instrument which is at the centre of the deeply felt human
need for music. This book, which can be carried and read,
opened and closed and reopened at the will of
fortunate owners is the gift of a lifetime.*'
ELIZABETH JOLLEY

A classical music guide
to life, love,
lust and other follies

SWOONING

CHRISTOPHER LAWRENCE

KNOPF

A Knopf Book
Published by Random House Australia Pty Ltd
20 Alfred Street, Milsons Point, NSW 2061
http://www.randomhouse.com.au

Sydney   New York   Toronto
London   Auckland   Johannesburg

National Library of Australia
Cataloguing-in-Publication Entry

Lawrence, Christopher.
Swooning: a classical musical guide to life, love, lust and other follies.

ISBN 1 74 051059 3

1. Music – Anecdotes. 2. Composers – Anecdotes.
3. Musicians – Anecdotes. 4. Music – Phychological aspects.
I. Title.

781.6802

Cover image: Ingres: *Odalisque with a Slave*, 1839–40 (Oil on
Canvas) Bridgeman Art Library
Jacket and internal design by Greendot Design
Typeset in 11.5/14 Bembo by J&M Typesetting,
Blackburn North, Victoria
Printed and bound by Tien Wah Press, Singapore

Every effort has been made to identify copyright holders of
extracts in this book. The publishers would be pleased to hear
from any copyright holders who have not been acknowledged.

10 9 8 7 6 5 4 3

For Linda

⊷ ACKNOWLEDGEMENTS ⊷

I'd like to thank Linda Siemon for her research assistance during both the writing and subsequent inspection of the manuscript;

Margaret Carter, who was kind enough to lend me her copy of J.B. Priestley's *Particular Pleasures* as an example of how classical music could be written about in a non-technical way;

The staff at the Café du Commerce in the southern French village of Sauve who looked away diplomatically as I wrote the book's initial treatment between sips of sauvignon blanc;

And Jeanne Ryckmans who summoned the book into existence and kept the author afloat with generous electronic applause.

ᏕWOONING

*A classical music guide
to life, love, lust and other follies*

⤍⤌ *Your Programme* ⤍⤌

Making Overtures

LOVE WITH VIOLINS
Hector Berlioz

LUST
Tutti

EXCESS & OBSESSION
Percy Grainger

TRIUMPH
Richard Wagner

JOY
Emmanuel Chabrier

ANGER
Ludwig van Beethoven

SADNESS
Peter Tchaikovsky

FREEDOM & RELEASE
Wolfgang Amadeus
Mozart

HOPE
Ross Edwards

PEACE
Hildegard of Bingen

➤⊶ *Coda* ⊷◄

This book should conclude by ten-thirty.

*It is requested that patrons do not swoon
in the aisles as this may distress
the performers.*

⊸ MAKING OVERTURES ⊶

*"Music was invented to deceive and
delude mankind."*
EPHORUS (4th century BC)

There's no denying it: music has this way of getting under one's skin. In the course of over two thousand years many writers have borne witness to its seductive power. Ever since rocks were banged in rhythm, lips pursed tentatively to bamboo, or attenuated strands of sheep gut strung within a wooden frame and plucked, music has been both pacifier and perverter of the power of reason. Why this should be so is a question that has never been answered satisfactorily. Even science is at a loss; Oliver Sacks recently remarked that writing and listening to music serves no evident evolutionary purpose. I wonder where this leaves bird song.

BUT WHAT IS IT? The difficulty for me is actually defining 'classical' music in the first place. Strictly speaking, it is Western European art music composed between 1750 and 1820. For many more people, it is 'old' music, mainly for orchestra, that takes too long to find a tune. A friend of mine, composer and writer Andrew Ford, described it recently as 'music that can stand on its own two feet'. I like this definition, because it implies an ongoing dynamism in music, rather than something that is stuck in time, getting more cobwebby by the day. If it's good, it is going to stick around. The Australian composer Ross Edwards (who stars in his own chapter — see **Hope**) says, '... there's no such thing as "new" music and "old" music; it's whatever music was and should be.' Now and forever, one hopes.

"Writing about music is like dancing about architecture."
ELVIS COSTELLO AND THELONIUS MONK

"There is nothing more difficult than talking about music."
CAMILLE SAINT-SAËNS (1835–1921)

These august gentlemen have a point. There *is* an irrelevance about trying to 'explain' music when music is 'about' something that words aren't. The world is full of maxims that concern music starting where the word leaves off.

Music is not literal. Many would maintain that music doesn't express anything at all. I disagree. Music is 'about' what it means to us; to be more precise, what it means to *you*. At that first hearing we intuitively relate it to various parts of our emotional selves. If we find that we can't do this, we lose patience with it and move on — for better or for worse. The actual responses can't be moulded, but the patience and application can — and this is where words about music can come in handy.

Words about music for the novice can be had in what is called a 'music appreciation' course. This is such an awful term. Learning to 'appreciate' good music is a bit like learning to sift patiently through your spouse's personality in search of the odd attractive feature in an arranged marriage. Of course many arranged marriages do work out, but only after the partners reach an accommodation with each other. These days we don't have the luxury of twenty years in which to learn to accommodate a Beethoven symphony.

What we're really after is fulfilment with some romance and excitement along the way. This is as true of people as it is of symphonies, sonatas and operas. We're not just encountering Beethoven; we're meeting him on a blind date. First impressions mean a lot. Eventually one learns to look (or listen) beneath the surface to the goodness within, but it helps to have been just a little captivated over the first dinner.

If religion is truly the opiate of the masses, then music is the cigarette holder. Its value as a tool of ritual is beyond question. Even on an individual basis the hypnotism works — at vulnerable moments of solitude, people can burst into spontaneous tears at the cue of a haunting refrain. At other times we may be persuaded by music's serenity to cast emotion aside in favour of the contemplation of less corporeal concerns. I can testify to this having happened on a daily basis for nearly five years while I presented a little segment on breakfast radio around Australia. Listeners were invited to tune in and *Swoon*.

The early morning pause for a *Swoon* quickly became … well, a ritual for many thousands of people. Toast would be served in time for eating along with something mellow. The scraping of the Vegemite would follow the slow rhythm of an ancient Armenian chant. Drivers would look dreamily at the car alongside as they queued up to pay the motorway toll. Commuters would linger at the wheel in the carpark at the end of the journey, windows wound up to seal in the faint burble of Venetian Baroque.

We had joked about serving a regular 'parcel of rapture', but the joke was on us; it seemed that we were performing a true public service, or at least fulfilling some deep need in many people. So deep, in fact, that they soon wanted more than weekday 'take-away'. It was time to give them Swoon on tap, and the first of the *Swoon* collections on CD was born.

We were rashly optimistic about the first of the *Swoon* collections and manufactured 5,000 copies for sale around Australia. Most classical releases sell a fraction of that figure but we hoped that regular radio exposure would give the CDs an extra kick along. It obviously helped: over four years that initial release was followed by two more and sales of the series have soared to well over a quarter of a million. Even assuming that the extra kick had turned into an almighty boot, this *Swoon* phenomenon had to have another explanation.

One reason for this success was undoubtedly the title, which signalled an appropriate mode of response. In show-biz parlance, it was the 'hook'. But that's not all. Most of us have some untouched emotional buttons hidden away. It should therefore come as no surprise that classical music can (ahem) play us like a violin. And how does this happen?

I believe that great music presents us with a sense of the universality of human experience; a reminder that when the composers were in full communicative flight they were, after all, talking about *us* — our longings, our desire for romance, our capacity for excess, and our wish for the eternal. The Reverend Sydney Smith described music as 'the only cheap and unpunished rapture upon earth'.

Why, then, do others find this music — the masterpieces of Beethoven, Bach, Mozart and the rest of the periwigged gang — so inscrutable when the conduct of the composers' own lives is resoundingly familiar? Granted, the craft of writing music requires great discipline. But take the composers away from their ink-splattered pages and the same old patterns of behavioural ineptitude begin to take shape. The capacity to write great music seems not to be a talent for living. Classical music — *nice*? Not at all. It is the most immediate expression of mental and emotional extremes; part deception (as Ephorus would have it), sometimes dangerous and frequently a discomforting revelation.

Just as the unsuspecting listener makes the connections between classical music and certain states of mind, so *Swooning: A classical music guide to life, love, lust and other follies* clusters fact, rumination and trivia into ten sections corresponding roughly with the sequence of emotions experienced in a love affair — one that doesn't work out. We're familiar with each of these stages — they bring out the best and worst in us — and music has derived much of its inspiration from them as well.

There is the unmistakable flavour of the scrap-book in the arrangement of material under these broad section headings. Each section also includes a close-up of a composer whose life exemplifies the emotional 'subject' in question. I should add that these biographies will not aim to be authoritative, being at best an anecdotal recounting of fact; neither is there an intention to try and name the ten 'best' composers. They are composers who have meant a great deal to me and to whose music I have been irresistibly drawn. In explaining the nature of that attraction I hope to provide guidance through example of developing a passion for classical music that will inspire the reader to chase up the music and life stories of other great composers.

Our cast of fellow sufferers in this book is drawn mainly

from the 'Romantic' period which ran through the nine-teenth century in Europe — they wanted emotion in music to be an art form, after all. Just one living composer is included, and it is only because I know him well that I feel I can speak about him with such arrant presumption.

What I *won't* do is tell you how you should listen to Tchaikovsky's Fifth Symphony, just as I won't try to tell you what, if anything, the Symphony is about, or indeed how Tchaikovsky went about writing it. That would be an attempt to write seriously about music, and in a funny way *Swooning* isn't really a book about music at all. Neither is it a book of philosophy. Philosophy tries to come up with solutions, whereas we'll just be looking at problems.

No — this is a book about **life**, or to be more specific, the feelings, tastes, aversions and cravings of an inner life. When we listen to great music, we juxtapose our life experience with that of the composer. The junction points that are created can bring us miraculously face-to-face with the people who've been good enough to send out musical messages.

So welcome to the wide, wild and wise world of classical music from the point of view of only one serious and life-long music lover. The orchestra has tuned, the lights in the hall have dimmed, and the conductor's baton signals the downbeat for the beginning of the romance. Settle back — it's telling you something …

⚘ LOVE WITH VIOLINS ⚘

*"Love cannot give an idea of music, but music can
give an idea of love."*
HECTOR BERLIOZ, 1865

That phrase is the inspiration for this book, so let
us begin our *Swoon* with that magic moment, when
eyes meet across a crowded room and — whoosh!
— you hear that orchestra. How Romantic — and
in the case of this French composer **Hector
Berlioz** (1803–1869), a maxim evolved from a lifetime's experience.

I FIRST HEARD the music of Berlioz when I was twelve. I'd
explored the family collection of Broadway musical sound-
tracks, Judy Garland concerts, Latin fizz like Herb Alpert
and Sergio Mendes, and early Beatles. My uninformed tin-
kerings at the piano were based on a cautious investigation
of some of Bach's kiddie stuff — the two-part inventions

and the odd simplified minuet. From there I began delving into classical music by scrounging money from my father to buy a cheap series of 10-inch LPs which came out each week under the title *The Great Composers*. An accompanying booklet detailed the composer's life.

It was his face that grabbed me. The portraits of the composers I'd seen in these booklets had displayed expressions ranging from complacent satisfaction to inner glow. These guys knew they were good and so, too, did the world. From this I concluded that talent inevitably earned universal approbation (maturity proved me wrong). Sure, Beethoven looked a little wild-eyed toward the end, but I figured that was the drink (see **Anger**).

Then came the Berlioz instalment. Wow, I thought, this guy's a little left-of-field: his name ends with a 'z'. And then I scanned to the record's cover portrait, which somehow had all the immediacy of a photograph. Painted in 1850 by Gustave Courbet, it shows a drawn face against a dark background. The mouth is tense. Deep-set eyes gaze warily, almost suspiciously, at the viewer. Even as a preteen, my physiognomical instincts told me this was not a happy man.

Hang on — this guy was probably a genius, I reasoned. With a brain like that, he should have been ecstatic. Being a kid in the euphoric (if not narcotic) '60s, it had never occurred to me that people had to Suffer for their Art. From what I'd seen, being talented in music or art meant that you could dress and behave strangely and be rewarded for this with money and celebrity. What was the Frenchman's problem?

The answer was on the disc. It was a symphony, but not a numbered piece like Beethoven's nine, Mozart's forty-one (at least) or Haydn's one hundred and four. No — this was called the *Symphonie fantastique* (or *Fantastic Symphony*), and each of its five movements also bore a title, beginning with *Rêveries — Passions*. Talk about a come-hither opener; being on the hormonal cusp of a bit of reverie/passion-mongering I was keen to hear what Berlioz had to say about it.

Pow! The piece started. I hope that everyone has the chance just once in their lives to feel that sort of connection with a creative artist that goes beyond mere aesthetic understanding or intellectual accord and arrives at something deeper: a real intuitive link, the sense that this person is singing your song as well as their own. The opening tune of the symphony is so suffused with longing — so *lonely* — that it shrugs off the comfort of any supporting rhythm. Even the accompaniment is cautious.

It seemed to me that Berlioz intended this music to be about *something*. For him, the opening was '… the expression of that overpowering sadness felt by a young heart first tortured by hopeless love'. I could go along with that. The Symphony was the soundtrack for some internal cinematic romantic drama for which Berlioz supplied a story or 'programme'. Even today it would satisfy the cravings of any dedicated tabloid reader:

HEADLESS MUSICIAN CONFRONTS WITCH GIRLFRIEND AT
DIABOLICAL ORGY AFTER DRUG OVERDOSE

And that's just the last two movements. No wonder they
loved it in Paris in 1830. This was the 'Fantastic' of the title.
Deep down, though, the Symphony is about love gone
wrong. Berlioz was writing from experience and, as many
of us do, he spent his life becoming an expert.

<hr />

Isn't it Romantic? One is tempted to think that the nineteenth century was one big musical 'love-in'. Love, in fact,
has a great deal to do with it. It represents the triumph of
the heart over the head, a shakeup of order. This is precisely
what a new generation of composers, artists and writers
were after in the early 1800s. For them, 'Romantic' con-
noted something wild, fanciful and strange. The conduct of
one's life could echo this new perception of Art: this was
also the era of the Extreme Reaction. One hundred and
thirty years before teenagers screamed and fainted at Elvis,
Berlioz and sundry other Paris-based passion heads like
Victor Hugo and Alexandre Dumas wept and vomited over
Shakespeare. The Bard's poetry gushed with the lava of real
life — even for those with little or no English.

Berlioz – Five Unhappy Love Stories

1816

Berlioz falls in love with Estelle (No.1), eighteen-year-old neighbour and family friend. There's nothing transient about this adolescent passion; she becomes one of the themes of his life. For the time being, there is no real future in this one; she thinks him merely cute. He's only twelve, after all.

1827

Now an impoverished music student, Berlioz attends performances of Shakespeare's *Hamlet* and *Romeo and Juliet* given by a visiting English company in Paris. (He later called this 'the supreme drama of my life'.) In a brain-altering two-way tackle Shakespeare reveals the true nature of Art while Irish actress Harriet Smithson (No.2), playing both Ophelia and Juliet has him instantly smitten. After *Romeo*, Berlioz allegedly leaves the theatre saying, 'I will marry that woman and write my greatest symphony on the play.' Good copy, but untrue. In the end, though, Berlioz does both.

1827- 1830

Obsession with Smithson takes on epic proportions. Berlioz behaves erratically and bores his friends. Stagedoor Johnny antics terrify the Irishwoman who warns others to 'beware the gentleman with the strange eyes'.

1830

Berlioz hears rumours that Smithson is sleeping with her manager. After emotional tempest and numerous long walks he writes the *Fantastic Symphony* in six weeks. He then falls for eighteen-year-old pianist Camille Moke (No.3). Requited lust a big factor here. They become engaged. Berlioz reluctantly leaves for Italy after winning a prestigious composition prize. The lovers exchange rings and vows of eternal constancy.

1831

Berlioz is told that Camille is to marry a wealthy piano manufacturer. He leaves for Paris with plans to execute simultaneous revenge murder/suicide in drag. He loses his frocks and resolve when his baggage goes missing *en route*. Change of plan: he jumps off a cliff into the sea. Splashing down near a fishing boat, he is conveniently rescued. Chastened, he writes a sequel to the *Fantastic Symphony* celebrating his return to life. It is called *Lélio, or The Return to Life*.

1832

Returns to Paris from Italy and discovers that Smithson is also back in town. He rents a room formerly occupied by the actress. Passion reawakens. The *Fantastic Symphony* and *Lélio* are performed at a concert in December. The Symphony's printed programme — the descriptions attached to the music — tells of a young man who overdoses because of unrequited love, but misjudges the dosage and instead experiences a series of hallucinations in which she is always present — the whirl of a ball, the isolation of the countryside, being driven to his own execution, and her transformation into a hag at a witches' sabbath. The 'beloved' in question is represented by a recurring theme — a 'fixed idea', or *idée fixe* — that all present in the 1832 audience know to be the emblem of Smithson herself. She attends the concert and is the subject of great attention. Afterwards she and Berlioz are formally introduced; a week later, they declare their love for each other.

1833

Harriet becomes Mrs Berlioz after a campaign of resistance from the composer's family. She is, after all, poor, Protestant, and an actress with a history.

1839

Berlioz composes his Dramatic Symphony, *Romeo and Juliet*.

1842

Marie Recio (No.4), a dark-eyed but untalented singer, becomes Berlioz's mistress. Harriet begins to slide into alcohol-fuddled despair.

1844

The Berlioz ménage finally splinters; 'the supreme drama' of his life is over. Marie is now his constant 'companion'.

1854

Harriet dies after a series of strokes. Liszt writes a letter of consolation to Berlioz: '… she inspired you, you loved her, you sang of her, her task was done.' Berlioz marries Marie Recio.

1862

Marie Recio dies suddenly from a heart attack. Berlioz falls in love with a mysterious woman less than half his age called Amélie (No.5).

1864

Getting a little grim now. Berlioz literally stumbles across Amélie's grave in the Montmartre cemetery. This is something of an unpleasant surprise, as you can imagine. Harriet's remains need to be relocated to make room for a new street in the modernised Paris and Berlioz witnesses her disinterment. He contemplates the now-detached head of his Ophelia/Juliet.

1864 - 1865

Berlioz decides to go back to No. 1 and resumes contact with Estelle, now in her late sixties. But the loop does not fully close. While he is finally able to declare his affection, she tells him essentially to cool off because she's now too old for that sort of thing. In his *Mémoires*, Berlioz resigns himself to adoring her from afar, calling her his 'distant star'.

***

It is a sad story. A man who gave his life to music and love felt at the end (with good cause) that he had been unsuccessful at both. Yet he could still write the quote at the head of this chapter, saying in addition:

"Love and Music are the two wings of the soul."

⸻

There is a song from the 1950s titled *All of a sudden, my heart sings*, and I can think of no better reason for the invention of **opera** in Italy circa 1594. Tragedy set to music was *de rigueur* in those days, but heck — it all comes back to love. In *L'Orfeo* (1607) by **Claudio Monteverdi** (1567–1643), the earliest opera to be still performed regularly, the eponymous musician of antiquity is widowed and vents his grief so persuasively (with music, of course) that at least one sentimental old god decides that Orpheus can nip down to the nether world, collect his wife and keep going as if nothing has happened. There is one string attached; he mustn't look at her during the trip back to earth. In opera everyone is too dim to follow their contract and so Orpheus sneaks a look. His wife drops dead (again). Orpheus promptly resumes whingeing and grieving. The gods, moved yet another time and no doubt anxious to shut Orpheus up once and for all, bring Eurydice back to life and reunite the pair. One wonders at the subtext today's psychologists would suggest for this story.

Love conquers everything in opera — even death itself, at times. Still, even the divine Monteverdi allowed sex to

16

drive the plot in opera by the end of his career. In his final opera *The Coronation of Poppea* (1642), a story of top-level high jinks in ancient Rome, the Emperor Nero casts aside his wife for a manipulative superior bonk. Not only do the baddies succeed and get away with it, they serenade their triumph in one of the most beautiful love duets ever written.

⚜

Love kills: Opera is a dangerous place for sopranos, mind you. High voices spend half the night tasting the pleasures of love only to find themselves dead by the end of the show. Forget about the supposedly ennobling aspects of high art; in the hands of someone like **Giacomo Puccini** (1858–1924), for instance, opera is a blood sport. Some highlights of the Diva Deathtoll:

Manon Lescaut (1893)

Soprano: Manon, a young girl.
Turpitude: Inflames the heart of student des Grieux. They decamp. Des Grieux runs dry of cash. Manon becomes the mistress of a treasurer-general,★ accepting jewels and frocks as compensation for older flesh. Continues to consort with des Grieux and tells treasurer-general she likes it this way.

Consequence paid: Manon dragged to jail as a thief. Eventually she is deported to Louisiana with a shipload of *filles de joie* (loose women).
Death: Dehydration, depression and exhaustion on a New Orleans plain.

*Note: Opera tends to stereotype politicians as middle-aged or older, wealthy, emotionally dysfunctional and manipulative. Surely nothing could be further from the truth.

La bohème (1896)

Soprano: Mimì, a seamstress.
Turpitude: Pops into garret of impoverished poet Rodolfo looking for a light. Fifteen minutes, two arias and a duet later, they are in love and Mimì is odds on to stay the night after a quick drink on the town. They move in together somewhere between Acts Two and Three.
Consequence paid: Ménage of emotional hell exacerbated by Rodolfo's concern for her health. Tearful separation. Mimì becomes the mistress of someone with more money.
Death: Tuberculosis. That nasty cough from Act One finally catches up with her.

Tosca (1900)

Soprano: Floria Tosca, fragrant diva in a sea of political intrigue.

Turpitude: Nuts about artistic type Cavaradossi who is friend and abettor of revolutionaries. He is captured by evil Scarpia, the Chief of Police, and interrogated under torture while Tosca watches. She agrees to Scarpia's terms: Cavaradossi's freedom in exchange for a bonk. As the Chief prepares to lower the britches, she stabs him to death with the famous line '… this is Tosca's kiss'.★

Consequence paid: What was to have been a mock execution of Cavaradossi by firing squad turns horribly real. Tosca ends up with a dead lover.

Death: Suicide, throwing herself from the top of a castle. Unlike the standard operatic death scene, Tosca does not sing on the way down.

★Note: Even real-life opera singers are given to extremes (see **Anger**).

Madam Butterfly (1904)

Soprano: Cio-Cio-San (Madam Butterfly), fifteen-year-old Japanese contract bride.

Turpitude: None, since she is an innocent and honourable girl who sticks to her contract. Taken as bride by visiting U.S. Navy Lieutenant who is clearly after a bit of passing

Oriental dumpling. Child conceived and born during Act One intermission. Lieutenant, ducking out for a loaf of bread, disappears for three years, during which time he takes a legitimate wife back in the States. Somewhat insensitively, the American couple find themselves back at Butterfly's place in Nagasaki.

Consequence paid: Love and honour are betrayed. Butterfly realises she was part of a lousy contract.

Death: Harakiri.

Sister Angelica (1918)

Soprano: Suor Angelica (Sister Angelica), nun.

Turpitude: Unmarried mother; not a good look in seventeenth-century Florentine aristocracy.

Consequence paid: Forced into nunnery and separated from child. She is later told by a disapproving aunt of the child's death.

Death: Suicide by home-brew poison. Audience begins to wonder when Puccini will give the soprano a break.

Turandot (1926)

Soprano: Liù, a young Chinese slave girl.

Turpitude: Not having title role, which has been taken by another soprano who is presumably collecting a bigger fee. Nevertheless, she loves the tenor.

Consequence paid: Consigned to pitiable 'girl next door' role; clearly will not get the tenor.
Death: Puccini's … leaving Act Three unfinished after having Liù commit suicide. The soprano's karmic revenge.

⁘

This is all larger than life stuff. For the true lover (as opposed to the fictional character onstage) something more intimate is required. Hence the **serenade** with its classic image of a besotted fellow in tights crooning up to the balcony of his girlfriend's room in the middle of a summer night — without waking the neighbours. The nocturnal al fresco confession of love was certainly popular by the late sixteenth century, if Shakespeare's *Romeo and Juliet* is any indication; the musical version was described in a German musical lexicon of 1732. The word itself derives from the Latin *serenus*, by the way. One imagines that the Latins thought of it first during a hot night. The weather is better in that part of Europe, after all.

Eventually the serenade became a much bigger deal, involving lots of instruments and more extended forms. The neighbours would have been furious, but by then balconies, girlfriends and starry skies had been taken out of the equation. Mozart wrote serenades for wind instruments (including his K.361, with its divine Adagio movement) and Brahms put in some early symphonic practice with a couple of serenades for orchestra.

If you are a courageous and mellow-voiced reader, you might like to consider the revitalisation of the serenade. I must confess that in my experience I've never heard it done successfully but this could be due to a bad choice of music. The classical composers provide serenades by the truckload: Mozart in several operas (*Don Giovanni* (1787), *The Abduction from the Seraglio* (1782), *Così fan tutte* (1790)), in Italian operas including those of Rossini and Donizetti, and in the cosier genres of art song and the parlour ballad, with very singable efforts by Schubert, Tosti and Mascagni. Really, any song composer worth their salt has bequeathed to us a romantic ditty or two worth having a crack at with a guitar. Of course, if your beloved lives above the second floor you may have to resort to a mobile phone.

One serenades with an ulterior motive. An invitation up to the balcony via the nearest trellis for a cup of chamomile tea perhaps, or a quick retune of the lute for a face-to-face duet in close harmony.

But back in the Middle Ages, circa the twelfth and thirteenth centuries, the French *troubadours* and *trouvères* went for more of a no-strings-attached serenade. They sang of **courtly love** (or as they called it in their time, *fin' amors*) which was more of a 'look, love, but don't touch' non-affair. To touch would not only have been a vulgar capitulation to sensual desire, but a breach of protocol; troubadours were supposed to love women above their station. Sometimes they could love them without actually having seen them; and when at last they set eyes on their ideal, could then swoon themselves to an early grave. That is at least how some contemporary accounts described it. It seems a little counter-productive somehow. A troubadour's love was expressed purely by the highest courtesy and a rich repertoire of poetry and song, some of the greatest of the time. There were hundreds of these fellows wandering around the courts of Europe, loitering behind columns and sublimating their love-sickness with a song every time they caught a passing whiff of rose petals. I'm surprised there were enough unattainable women to go around. Fragrant longing was the style; one only maintained a presence in those exalted corridors by being 'courteous and accomplished'. If you wanted raunchier stuff, you had to go to the monasteries (see **Lust**).

But will it last? As the counsellor would say — it depends on how much you have in common. For those who want to take their love down the aisle, our cast can offer some useful precedents:

Take care with actresses: Classic mistake for those with theatrical aspirations. Hector Berlioz and Harriet are explained in sorry detail above. Richard Wagner's first marriage to Minna Planer had a rocky start and only spluttered back to life when he or she wasn't involved with someone else at the time (see **Triumph**). The conductor **Leopold Stokowski** (1882–1977) enjoyed a much-publicised liaison with Greta Garbo in the 1930s, fuelled mainly by his curiosity about making love to a lesbian. He later said it was wonderful. In the 1902 opera *Adriana Lecouvreur* by Cilea we have a Count and a Prince in love with duelling actresses. Adriana herself eventually succumbs to the fatal scent of poisoned violets sent by her rival. They really can be so nasty to each other.

Singers are a better bet: One would have thought a diva to be dangerous, but there is evident domestic happiness to be had with a soprano. Classical music's perfect match could well be that of Norwegian composer **Edvard Grieg** (1843–1907) and his wife — also his cousin! — Nina. They married young and remained blissfully happy and serene for the next forty years. He wrote songs for her; she sang them at their joint recitals. Just a few years before he predeceased her, Grieg wrote: '… once in my life I was endowed with genius. The genius was Love.' Opera composers were likewise attracted to the living incarnations of their muse: Verdi's second wife and Rossini's first were loving and long-term companions. The German **Richard Strauss** (1864–1949) married soprano Pauline de Ahna in 1894 and presented four of his best songs to her as a wedding gift. She would appear to have worn the pants at home; Strauss once confessed to Mahler, 'My wife's a bit rough, but that's what I need.' Closer to our own time, the relationship between **Benjamin Britten** (1913–1976) and tenor **Peter Pears** (1910–1986) was the direct inspiration of some of the greatest vocal and operatic music of the twentieth century.

The second time around: Love can indeed be lovelier with a rerun. Other composers have made a much better go of it than Berlioz; the great Father **Bach** (Johann Sebastian), for instance, who enjoyed a happy and fruitful marriage to his second cousin, Maria Barbara, until her early death in 1720, leaving Johann with a few little Bachs to feed. (He was an enthusiastic and tireless baby-maker.) Wife number two was Anna Magdalena, who at the age of only twenty — sixteen years younger than the composer — was obviously going to match him baby for baby. They started with a new one each year, eventually relaxing the pace a little as Bach moved into his mid-fifties, and although the mortality rate was high (the norm for the early eighteenth century) at any given time there would have been ten children running around the house. The dutiful Anna Magdalena (a former singer) even kept a hand-written music-book for the kiddies' musical studies. Many of the Bach boys became composers. Likewise Verdi, Shostakovich, Rossini and Stravinsky enjoyed great luck at the second attempt after being widowed, even though the latter two were merely marrying their long-time mistresses. Mozart was rejected by one Aloysia Weber (a singer!) before opting to fall in love and marry her younger sister Constanze. A good, lustful marriage (see **Lust**).

...And then some: The itinerant piano virtuoso and composer **Henry Litolff** (1818–1891) was enthusiastic about marriage but not a great stayer. Early keenness was shown in his elopement at the age of seventeen with his soon-to-be first wife when she was only sixteen. They separated not long after but his attempts over the next few years to secure a divorce were unsuccessful; one of them resulting in a heavy fine and a spell in an English prison (from which he escaped after sweet-talking the wife of one of the wardens). Two more marriages and divorces followed. Finally, in his late fifties, he took as his fourth wife a seventeen-year-old girl who had been his nurse during a period of illness. She continued in this role for his remaining fifteen years.

A note for wives: Apropos the above, remember this — he may look intense and display an attractively mercurial temperament now, but you could be in for trouble further down the track. **Robert Schumann** (1810–1856) and his wife Clara Wieck were married after what is possibly the most famous and dramatic romance in music: she, the brilliant and wilful daughter of Schumann's piano teacher; he, a bundle of nervous energy that bordered on the manic. Clara was a teenage piano prodigy; Robert was a promising player whose ambitions were foiled abruptly after he maimed a finger on his right hand with a bizarre contraption he'd invented to help him with his practice. Clara's father did all he could to poison the liaison; letters, slanders and legal proceedings. Love triumphed and the pair were married the day before Clara's twenty-first birthday in September 1840. Their bliss was punctuated by Robert's depressions and breakdowns. In 1854 he threw himself into the Rhine River after complaining of the taunting voices of devils interrupting his sleep. He spent the next two-and-a-half years in an asylum without seeing his wife or their children. Clara set eyes on him again the day before he died, probably of self-starvation.

Jelka Rosen, the wife of **Frederick Delius** (1862–1934) was also taking on a handful, given that he'd long been infected with syphilis when they married in 1903. Twenty years later he was blind, paralysed and confined to a wheelchair. The strain of his care must have been immense and although she never contracted the disease from her husband Jelka's health declined almost as fast as his and she died less than a year after him.

⚜

Love songs: A great hit from **Claudin de Sermisy** (c1490–1562) was his chanson *Tant que vivray*, which translates 'As long as I live in my prime/I shall serve the mighty king of Love'. This was arranged for all sorts of vocal and instrumental combinations and appeared in publications right through until 1644.

⚜

Instruments of Love:

The flute

> The soft complaining flute
> In dying notes discovers
> The woes of hopeless lovers ...
>
> John Dryden, *A Song for St Cecilia's Day* (1687)

The cello

> The cello is like a beautiful woman who has not grown older, but younger with time, more slender, more supple, more graceful.
>
> Pablo Casals, *Time* magazine (1957)

Sympathetic vibrations: The **viola d'amore** (or 'viola of love') was a kind of viola popular during the seventeenth and eighteenth centuries. These days, the members of the violin family that one hears in symphony orchestras sport only four strings apiece, but this sexy old voluptuary with a whiff of the Middle East about her sound has no fewer than fourteen; seven playing strings and another seven underneath which resonate in sympathy. A gentle swipe of the bow and — kerpow! — sonic coercion. There is also an **oboe d'amore** in the woodwind family; the name referring to the sound of the instrument rather than the means of its production. A pity, really; a wind instrument requiring two sets of lips for its operation may well have been popular.

Richard Wagner fell in love with his future wife Cosima when she accepted his offer of a lift back to a hotel in an empty wheelbarrow.

For a final word on the subject we should return to Berlioz. It reveals a streak of cynicism that always remained within his psyche; or is it mere pragmatism? In the final song of his cycle about love called *Les Nuits d'été* (Summer Nights), a traveller asks to be taken to the place where love lasts forever.

'Alas,' says the boatman, 'no such place exists.'

For the sake of this book's premise, we'll assume that the relationship has passed through this glorious start. From uncomplicated matters of the heart the music now takes us downward to a darker mood … and another part of the anatomy.

LUST

*"I slept with that woman for seven years. Wouldn't
you think that she'd remember that I hate fish?"*

ARTURO TOSCANINI
to a friend after being served caviar by a former mistress

NOTICE FOR BOOKSHOP BROWSERS

Oh, come on now. I know exactly why you're here. You've
had a good ogle at the woman on the front cover and then
snatched a look at the spine to see if her naughty bit is
obscured by lettering. I expect you're a man. You think you
can pick up this book like any common Fanny Hill paper-
back and cut straight to the sexy bits without flashing so
much as a credit card? How dare you; you go right back to
the first chapter so that we can begin this relationship on a
decent footing. You'll get to **Lust** in good time. Otherwise
you should put this down and try yourself out on the
'Women in Sport' coffee-table epic two aisles away. There
are no pictures here.

In any case, classical music is about the 'finer things'. We come to Johann Sebastian Bach when the clamour of the material world and the roaring of the hormones has died down. If you're into genitals, try painting or sculpture. Or contemporary film and theatre. Or Henry Miller. You'll find nothing like that in Mozart (or so you think).

So off you go then. Put this down or pay up … or flick across to **Peace**.

Now that you're here as a bona fide reader, please disregard the above. This chapter should really be called 'Sex' — **Lust** being merely a coy attempt to circle around the main thrust of the material. Perhaps one should be more up front about such matters. In doing so, one is simply following the lead of the composers themselves.

The history of music is a hormonal one. Sex looms large in opera plots, in the success or failure of musical careers, in the psychology of performers and composers, and (according to some) the very contours of music itself. Sex in classical music has confused the censors and either stimulated or outraged audiences. Morals have been affronted and bosoms set heaving. We even describe music as 'ravishing', as if it were a passionate lover.

Sexually transmitted diseases darkened or ended the lives of the greats (Schumann, Chabrier, Donizetti, Schubert and Delius — to name a few). Bach's twenty-plus children and

Mozart's explicit letters to his wife are proof of their vigorous marriages. Many other musicians shopped around. For performers then as now it was a life 'on the road'. Liszt was popular for more than merely flashing a mean arpeggio. One of Liszt's illegitimate daughters pursued a long and famous adulterous relationship with Wagner before their eventual marriage (see **Triumph**). In the turbulent world of musical theatre, adultery usually arrives just before intermission.

Classical music — *nice*? What a load of codswallop. Take Mozart, for instance. Quite apart from being a rebel for his time in the late eighteenth century (see **Freedom & Release**) there was a lot more surging beneath Mozart's livery than the next opera. Even some of his operas have plots driven by sex. At the very beginning of *The Marriage of Figaro* (1786) one hero is seen measuring up the space available for the nuptial bed. *Così fan tutte* is an exercise in partner-swapping. *Don Giovanni*, which, like *Figaro*, is set to a libretto by the seemingly priapic Lorenzo da Ponte, a good friend of Casanova, features as its anti-hero an insatiable aristocrat whose conquests run into the thousands. Mozart calls it a *dramma giocoso* — a sort of jolly drama. I propose a similar approach in a section that could easily be either too grim or too salacious in tone. We don't need a central composer figure in **Lust**, unlike the other chapters, because, let's face it, everyone was doing it.

Caught in flagrante: Sex killed **Alessandro Stradella** (1639–1682), one of the most famous Italian composers of his time, but disease or exhaustion were not factors in his demise. He paid the ultimate price for repeatedly ignoring a maxim that holds true to this day: don't filch your employer's merchandise.

Stradella first hit trouble in his native Rome in 1669 when he tried to embezzle money from the Roman Catholic Church in company with a corrupt abbot and a violinist. In the ensuing scandal the young composer left town. It was the first of several quick exits.

One such scamper to Venice dropped Stradella in it even further. He was hired by a member of a powerful local family, one Alvise Contarini, to teach music to his mistress. Music soon proved the food of something and Stradella decamped with his pupil. Never cross a Venetian; the out-raged Contarini gathered forty henchmen and tracked his traitorous music teacher to Turin with vengeance on his mind. Stradella was saved by the diplomatic protection of a friendly local regent, but Contarini slipped some *scudi* to two more assassins who made an attempt on the composer's life in October 1677. Legend has it they were going to ambush him after a concert of his music in Rome, but finding his work so much to their taste they instead intro-duced themselves, complimented Stradella on his gorgeous oratorio and advised him to get the hell out of there. What a sentimental old pair of back-stabbers. You don't see too many hired killers with a refined aesthetic sense these days.

Stradella's brains stayed firmly in his britches, even after such warnings. In early 1682 in Genoa he was at it again — this time with a young woman 'connected' with the Lomellini family. He really should have stuck to tavern wenches. This was the final straw. The soldier who was set upon him was obviously less partial to sonatas. Stradella was stabbed to death in a piazza.

<hr>

A more immediate post-coital death was inflicted upon the wife of the slightly mad and exceedingly angry Prince of Venosa, **Don Carlo Gesualdo** (1561–1613). She had been amusing herself with the Duke of Andria, unaware that her husband had got wind of the affair. It would seem that seventeenth-century Italians didn't handle this sort of thing very well. One evening when Mrs G. and her cavalier were savouring the proverbial cigarette, secure in the belief that Don Carlo was away inspecting his estates, the seething Prince burst into the bedroom armed with a gun and a deadly stiletto knife. The former he emptied into the Duke, while the latter was employed on his wife in a precursor to the shower scene from *Psycho*. He eventually tired of murdering and became a composer of madrigals that still sound weird today.

A Message for Gentlemen Readers

Ever find the discipline of monogamy too burdensome? Do the exploits of a Don Juan or a Casanova make you just a tad envious? If so, you'll find a vicarious pleasure in Mozart's 1787 opera *Don Giovanni*. The Don is a Spanish nobleman who simply cannot have enough women. And when the persuasion of rank or charm are not enough, force will have to do. He commits a rape and a murder in the first five minutes but becomes more charming as time goes on — or perhaps, he just seems to as the master psychologist Mozart drags us down to the Don's level. Certainly there is plenty of ringside action as we observe him with three women on the trot and a fourth in his sights in Act Two.

This all takes place over a mere couple of days and the rate of conquest has been maintained for some time. We discover this through the statistics offered by the Don's servant Leporello in the famous 'Catalogue' Aria. Notches in the bedhead would have turned his furniture to woodchips so Leporello makes entries in a ledger according to nationality. It includes 640 Italian women, 231 German fräulein, 100 French mesdames, a rather lacklustre 91 Turks, but in his home hunting ground of Spain 1,003 and counting (there is something gruesomely comic about this number just trickling into the four figures).

The aria illustrates the pathology and the techniques of the sexual compulsive: fair-haired women are praised for their kindliness, brunettes for their constancy, blondes for their 'sweetness' (rather than their intelligence, you'll note).

The Don calls tall women 'majestic' and short women 'dainty'. His indiscriminate tastes make him very PC. Every age, shape and social class is fair game; for instance, plump women are preferred during the colder months. This is 1787 and electric blankets are a long way off. But observe the date and marvel at Mozart's prescience. The French Revolution and the beginning of the end of the aristocracy is just around the corner, crowds roaring in triumph as uncomprehending and unrepentant nobility met the guillotine. Mozart uses the Don's rampant genitals as a symbol of all that is wrong with his world. At least, that is what I suspect he's doing. It would be a pity if a sexual enthusiast like Mozart was going a little prudish on us by suggesting that all dashing ladies' men with too much petrol in the tank go to Hell. For that is the fate that befalls Don Giovanni at the end of the opera.

The Danish premiere of Mozart's *Don Giovanni* took place in 1807 with the Swiss-born Edouard Dupuy, also a composer, in the lead role. He seems to have taken the part to heart. When later employed at the Royal Court to teach singing to the Princess Consort of Prince Christian Frederik — later Christian VIII — the pupil ill-advisedly fell in love with her teacher. Both were exiled, ending his career in that country.

⋘⋙

Wolfgang and his 'little boy': Mozart himself was nothing like the Don: he was low-born, frequently short of cash (but not as destitute as legend would have it), and was not promiscuous. On the other hand, he was not an abstainer and it is refreshing to read of his continuing lust for his wife, Constanze. As he wrote to his father, '... her whole beauty consists of two little black eyes and a beautiful figure'. One notes that her intelligence was not praised by her husband-to-be. Constanze was a nice, kind girl who happened to turn Wolfgang on. He was twenty-five and frisky. She was frisky as well. The engagement almost fell apart when she allowed a strange man to measure her calves during a party game. Mozart presumably claimed first dibs on her calves although his real interest lay further north. In his letters on tour he confessed to her of his longing for her backside and for her 'dear little nest', a receptacle for his 'little boy' which, even as he writes (in 1789), '... sneaks onto the table and looks at me enquiringly'. This has nothing to do whatsoever with his subsequent opera *The Magic Flute* (1791).

⋘⋙

Cafarelli and his Magic Flute: I must confess to a misapprehension about the castrati of the eighteenth century. They were a breed of male glamour singer much sought after by the leading composers of opera and the subject of adulation by audiences. Their voices soared with the almost unearthly purity of a boy soprano because that is effectively what they were; their pre-pubescent range having been retained thanks to surgical intervention. A quick nip here and there, two faint plops in a jar and hey presto! … one was high for life, the boyish notes amplified by a grown man's frame.

Adulation by fans often gave way to fascination, as shown in a recent film about the most famous castrato of them all — **Farinelli** (1705–1782). (They often sported single stage names, rather like today's fashion designers or hypnotists.) The singer's non-vocal displays on-screen also corrected a lifelong misapprehension of mine; I had always thought that with a couple of jacks removed from the deck, offering a full house was impossible. This was understandable, given that it had been ages since my last discussion with a eunuch on the subject of virility. In fact the castrati could delight their more ardent admirers with all the confidence of a walking contraceptive.

The vigorous **Caffarelli** (aka Gaetano Majorano, (1710–1783)) certainly did. He was one of Europe's favourites, serenading French dauphines through the latter stages of their pregnancies, and premiering the title role in **George Frideric Handel's** (1685–1759) opera *Serse* (Xerxes) (1738) — the famous aria *Ombra mai fu*, known as Handel's *Largo*, was written for him. The virtuoso singer once shared a stage with a live elephant and several camels, upstaging all of them.

Caffarelli's was the true prima donna temperament. He was thrown in prison in 1741 for making indecent gestures at the audience during an opera performance and had earlier been under house arrest after attacking a colleague in a Naples church while a nun was taking the veil. For certain female admirers of his voice he was happy to offer proof of the knife-hewn pudding. In Rome in 1728 he was surprised *in flagrante delicto* by a returning husband and forced to spend the rest of the night hiding in a disused water tank. Anxious not to go the way of a Stradella (see above), Caffarelli's mistress hired bodyguards to protect the singer from her husband's revenge for the rest of his stay.

It is such a relief to learn of ribaldry in people whom we esteem. All those juices have to go somewhere and it would be a shock if the tip of the quill alone proved a sufficiently wide conduit. Personally, I loathe the puritanism we try to attach to composers. A listener to my old radio programmes once complained to a newspaper letters column that when I spoke about Mozart I was 'vulgar' (see **Freedom & Release**). Presumably she never read what Mozart had to say about Mozart, who was the Les Patterson of back-door jokes. One shouldn't disassociate this from his compositional process; he was the greater composer for it. Strangely, we don't expect artists or writers to be such cleanskins. A painter can be acclaimed for a rendition of women's breasts but if a composer writes an opera about them (as the Frenchman **Francis Poulenc** (1899–1963) did in 1947 — *The Breasts of Tiresias*) it is dismissed as 'absurd'.

<hr/>

Sex in opera: This is a whole book in itself. Aldous Huxley once quoted an Italian proverb: 'Bed is the poor man's opera'. The Italians should know; they invented the genre in the late 1500s. One could invert the phrase and say with confidence that opera has been the rich man's bed. Opera plots are full of wealthy, powerful and sometimes geriatric men coveting sexual favours from younger women.

Interestingly, the women can use their allure to manipulate the situation to their advantage. In Puccini's *Tosca*, the beautiful opera singer knows that the chief of police, Baron Scarpia, wants more than just her arias and allows him to think he has won before administering her famous 'kiss'. The nubile Salome in Richard Strauss' opera (first performed in 1905) is quite prepared to drop all seven of her veils for the sexually demented Herod so that she can pucker up. That the object of her desire turns out to be John the Baptist's severed head proves that opera is best taken after dinner. In *Lulu* by Alban Berg (Acts One and Two first performed in 1937), the *femme fatale* collects a form of Scarpia's revenge when she finds herself on the wrong end of Jack-the-Ripper's knife at the opera's end.

On a happier note, the maid Serpina ('little snake' in Italian) tricks her way into marrying her wealthy and elderly employer Uberto in Giovanni Pergolesi's *La serva padrona*, or 'The Maid as Mistress' (1736). One suspects these same techniques have been used since.

***

Stop Press: An interesting plot line in the Frenchman **Darius Milhaud's** (1892–1974) mini-opera *The Rape of Europa* (1927) ... Europa ends her relationship with Pergamon upon discovering her love of animals. He is, understandably, furious.

***

When the composer and piano virtuoso Franz Liszt played in Berlin in 1842, the audience went bananas. Adoring women collected the broken strings from the pianos at the end of his recitals and had them converted into bracelets. Other cast-offs became souvenirs: coffee dregs were preserved in perfume bottles and cigar butts were lovingly hidden in cleavages. The term 'Lisztomania' was invented to describe the phenomenon.

***

'Stop that modern movement': Ah, the waltz — respectable incarnation of the romance and style of old Vienna! That is how we think of it these days. But the whirling dance in triple time involving close contact broke through the strangulated body language of early nineteenth-century Europe like an obscene gesture. The advent of the waltz in England in 1790 inspired the press to compare it to copulation. A duel was fought by a general and a young fop over its acceptability; shots were fired but bodies, souls and feet were spared. At last, an acceptable choreographic grope. Lord Byron — in a rare instance of prudery — published an anti-waltz poem under a pseudonym:

> Hot from the hands promiscuously applied,
> Round the slight waist, or down the glowing side …
> The breast thus publicly resigned to man
> In private may resist him — if it can.
> 'Horace Hornem, Esq.',
> *The Waltz: An Apostrophic Hymn* (1813)

───

Just what is all the fuss about Ravel's *Bolero*? Even before Dudley Moore and Bo Derek used it as a love-making aid in the 1979 film *10* the work had somehow earned a reputation as classical music's ultimate aphrodisiac. But with the film's success the *Bolero*'s exotic power became legend and every self-respecting Lothario kept a recording along with incense and a mirror over the bed.

Written as a ballet score in 1928 for Ravel's friend Ida Rubinstein and her ballet troupe, the original scenario does carry a strong undercurrent of sex — a young woman dancing alone in a dim Spanish café to an audience of men — but since then the piece has made its way to the concert platform, creating its own sensual aroma without the help of pictures. It began getting under people's skins almost immediately; even during Ravel's lifetime it was used in a 1934 Paramount film called *Bolero* that starred Carole Lombard and George Raft.

We're often told that artists create from direct experience. In this instance it is difficult to associate the sinuous and apparently orgasmic writhings of the *Bolero* with the persona of its composer. Ravel, in short, was not a raver. Diminutive, secretive and impeccably dressed, it appears unlikely that he ever spoiled the perfect creases in his trousers by lowering them for anybody.

Ravel called it 'seventeen minutes of orchestration without music' and 'an experiment in a special and limited direction'. If this sounds like a description of a score in handcuffs one has to acknowledge that there is a whiff of bondage about it: one tune, one rhythm, no development. The basic materials are bound, gagged and tortured in Chinese-water style by the ceaseless tapping of a snare-drum. (Kinky.) Each time that unchanging tune comes around there are a few more instruments involved, making one long crescendo. The thrust is the same; only the equipment gets bigger. Finally the harmony explodes into another key but the ropes stay on — nobody is going to stop that bloody drum. A couple more bangs and it's over. Where, I ask you, was the foreplay? Couldn't we have tried another position (key signature)? That's it; seventeen minutes? Most importantly, why doesn't Ravel offer us a cigarette?

This is not to disparage the *Bolero*'s undeniable impact. Like any talented lover it almost demands a standing ovation after each performance. But as in most of the meanings we 'perceive' in music, its sexual allure is our own collective projection from the less-frequented parts of our erotic natures. Ravel's music was criticised in his time for being 'reptilian' and 'cold-blooded'. It seems that some of us like the idea of a short one-night stand with a stranger in snakeskin.

***

Many years ago I was producing a recording of Ravel's *Bolero* with the Sydney Symphony Orchestra. The conductor Stuart Challender noted with some amusement that our recording date for this porcelain potboiler of musical erotica was St Valentine's Day. We all put in a hard morning's work re-recording 'patches' of the work before our final take — number 69.

Imputing erotic meaning to the *Bolero* seems wasteful when many other composers are happy to provide more explicit commentary. In **Claude Debussy's** (1862–1918) *Prelude to the Afternoon of a Faun* (1894) our cloven-footed hero is cavorting with a bevy of naked nymphs (according to Stéphane Mallarmé's original poem). Or is he just dreaming about it? That's the faun's flute at the start, by the way. Scriabin's *The Poem of Ecstasy* (1908) evokes copulation on a cosmic scale, describing the union of the 'male Creator-Spirit and the Woman-World'. The orchestra is appropriately huge for this heavyweight encounter with a solo trumpet in the lead role of the Phallus. This is the only orchestral piece I know about multiple orgasms. Scriabin originally called it 'The Orgiastic Poem'.

For a terrific musical orgy you can do no better than the final bacchanale of the ballet *Daphnis and Chloé* (1912), by (here he is again) Ravel. The story is simple: boy meets girl, girl abducted by pirates, pirates frightened by an apparition of the god Pan, girl and boy reunited and all celebrate. Listen to the chorus as they whoop and pant in rhythm over the whirring orchestra. Don't tell me they're just playing cards. This supple and voluptuous score leaves *Bolero* in the shade for sex appeal.

Back on the home playing field, one can't overlook **Richard Strauss'** (1864–1949) *Domestic Symphony* (1903), a portrait of the pleasures to be had with the family. According to the programme — or written narrative illustrated by the music — Strauss has spent the evening playing with his child. The clock strikes seven and the composer and his wife retire. A 'Love Scene' ensues before the clock strikes seven the next morning. It was a while before Strauss was again as wholesome as this: his next major work was the opera *Salome* (1905).

If all this keeping the ears open for sexuality in music seems too puerile or voyeuristic, rest assured that it is in fact a respectable academic exercise. The eminent Sir George Grove wrote in the first edition of his *Dictionary of Music and Musicians* (1882) that '... compared with Beethoven, Schubert is as a woman to a man'. There are all sorts of implications that stem from this ambiguous comparison and present-day musicologists haven't wasted the opportunity. The repeated 'wham-bam-bams' at the end of Beethoven's symphonies have been likened to an insistence on always being on top (have a listen to the end of the Ninth, for instance). Schubert's more 'feminine' musical attributes remarked upon by Grove have recently been extrapolated into an imprint of gayness. Poor Schubert; outed by his crotchets. I'm not particularly interested in these arguments and would love to see them refuted by unexpected evidence — a lithograph of Beethoven in a frock, for instance. Composers' sexual orientation doesn't shout out to me as a decisive element in classical music appreciation and you'll have noticed this hasn't been a kiss-and-tell chapter in that regard — although I was fascinated to learn that Tchaikovsky and Saint-Saëns once danced a *pas de deux* on the empty stage of the Moscow Conservatory (more on Tchaikovsky later).

␥

The American soprano **Mary Garden** (1874–1967) stirred many a male opera fan's loins, being unusually svelte by diva standards of the day. An elderly admirer, staring at her décolletage, asked what kept her strapless dress up.

'Your age, sir,' she replied.

␥

The outpourings of randy and dipsomaniacal medieval monks are captured in *Carmina Burana*, set to music in 1935–36 by the German **Carl Orff** (1895–1982). Its opening chorus, *O Fortuna*, is one of classical music's most identifiable anthems because of its frequent use in television commercials and movie trailers; there's a wild, almost heathen nature to its surging chant about the capriciousness of Fate — the mob speaks. Early on the chorus confesses its desire to lie in the arms of the Queen of England. This is well before the Elizabeths, of course.

The final word: Sex sells? Recent discussion on the 'crisis' in classical music reveals the pomposity that always attaches to any discussion of so-called 'high' and 'low' art. We don't really know what distinguishes the two; nevertheless we become extremely upset if we suspect they've been mixed together.

The great composers occupy lofty positions in our pantheon of Western achievement. Nothing gets much 'higher'. But they're not unassailable, it seems; some of those lily-white countenances have begun to bear the dirty fingerprints of rapacious marketeers. That at least is the chorus of complaint from some anxious cultural observers.

It goes something like this: in an orgy of profit-mongering and desecration, poor Mozart and Beethoven have been allowed to consort with pouting hussies who occasionally let their bare breasts get in the way of a good performance. Entire symphonies and concertos have been carved up by CD compilations and certain radio stations and the bleeding chunks offered to a public newly racked by short concentration spans for ease of consumption. Dear old Father Bach, who spent a productive lifetime writing music 'for the glory of God', now provides a mere background accompaniment for the more mundane glories of cocktail tippling, supermarket browsing and perhaps even the odd naughty.

Even your humble writer has been accused of cheapening the message of the masters through the success of the

Swoon compilations based on the popular segment in my radio breakfast show years ago. They sold by the truckload — far in excess of all our expectations — and did so without trespassing into the traditional 'greatest hits' territory. We simply collated the music from the *Swoon* segments that had elicited the greatest listener response. The results were a testimony to the natural eclecticism of people who love good music, ranging from old Armenian chant to new-age settings of old Gaelic texts; from a Canadian dance-hall tune to a contemporary Australian violin concerto by Ross Edwards (see **Hope**). They were (and are) a collection of private arcana, about as far from the formulaic second-guessing of public taste as a sheltered and marketing-blind public servant such as myself can get.

But when the sales figures moved into the stratosphere normally occupied by successful pop music releases, fuelled more by word of mouth than any massive (and for us, unaffordable) promotional campaign, I noticed some murmurs of discontent in the quiet of the high temple. If almost anyone was buying a *Swoon* CD, it stood to reason that I had abused this wonderful material with some dreadful 'low art' approach. I recall having to sit smiling at a classical CD awards night while a newspaper music critic and retired academic took the microphone to intone his disapproval of compilations 'titled with a single word'. Since mine was the only one that had come out that year nobody was in any doubt as to the identity of the accused. Apparently a single-word description — or to be even more vulgar, 'branding' — of 'high-art' music trivialises it by stealing away its indefinable, non-verbal message and complexity of approach. It makes a bland suggestion to the listener as to how he or she should respond. If they're gullible enough to follow, then they're not the sort of person who should be listening to the stuff in the first place. You and I are therefore complicit in a vast public idiocy, or as it has been described, a 'crisis' of commercialism.

According to this argument, the record companies are the ones leading the hordes to the temple gates with their mass-market imperatives. The writer Norman Lebrecht, in his recent book *When the Music Stops* appends the subtitle *… the corporate murder of classical music*. It's all been Coca-Colised, he claims; talent is subordinate to looks, worthiness to expediency and a fast buck. The young are in. I'm always suspicious of people who whinge about an increasing predilection for youth; it usually means that the complainant is simply getting older. There *is* a new wave of, say, young female violinists who look appealing on CD covers — Leila Josefowicz, Hilary Hahn and Anne-Sophie Mutter, for instance — and they can all certainly play a mean fiddle. Jascha Heifetz played a mean fiddle as well but he theoretically wouldn't get a look in today unless he looked as fetching as Mutter in a strapless dress.

Of course there have been some deliberate attempts to make sales through titillation. Vanessa-Mae has posed for covers in wet T-shirts and hot-pants, and has sold well too (not, I suspect, by dragging potential buyers away from Jascha Heifetz). Linda Brava generated publicity by appearing only with her violin in *Playboy* magazine. There have been innumerable cleavages (this is where sopranos come into their own) and the odd male bicep on compilations that feature gay, or allegedly gay, composers. I think there was even a nipple on one of the Swoon CDs; admittedly from a nineteenth-century painting, but hey! the accusation stands. Sex has been let loose in classical music's sacred precinct.

In fact the only thing new in classical music is this wowserish puritanism. If there is one lesson you'll have learned from this chapter it is that sex has been present in classical music all along. I doubt this brutal discovery means that you love it less; in fact, your understanding of it can only increase. It would be perverse if such a vital element of life were to be miraculously absented from musical expression. And yet that is what the culture of 'classical' music appreciation has attempted to do, particularly since the time of Beethoven. The gift of musical inspiration is supposed to be 'divine', coming from a higher plane (as when composers talk about waiting for an idea, or the music flowing through them). Sex and base human instinct don't exist up there so therefore great music has no truck with them — it is about 'finer things'.

Classical music *is* often about these 'finer things', it's true — you'll discover this later in the book as our progression of a love affair's emotions moves towards resolution and closure. But the music is also about us; all our light and shade, our earthly yearnings and denials, including those below the waist. That is why we can let all this purist disquiet pass us by. Frankly, the old temple could do with a bit of graffiti and a few more salacious photos. If cleavage proves as much an incentive as the name 'Schubert' in having a CD plucked off a shelf for inspection, I imagine the composer and his music are big enough to withstand the juxtaposition. Irrelevant images may be too pervasive but they're also ephemeral. In my broadcasting experience, the intelligence of most of those new to the musical classics makes them very quick to separate the talent from the tits.

⇥ EXCESS & OBSESSION ⇤

"Indulged in to excess, music emasculates instead of invigorating the mind."
PLATO (429–347 BC), *The Republic*

"Apart from sex I am not such a bad fellow. But … I am not really interested in anything else."
PERCY GRAINGER, 1956

"I smoke. I drink. I stay up all night. I screw around. I'm overcommitted on all fronts."
LEONARD BERNSTEIN, 1986

When too much is a necessity: Don't think I'm parading these as negative qualities. After all, nobody really does anything well unless they feel compelled to do it repeatedly; compulsion breeds a stronger discipline than mere obligation. **Obsession is the fuel of excellence.** And excess? Sometimes we need to crash through the walls of our own experience if we are ever going to know what lies beyond, since most of us are reluctant to open the door. These are hardly new thoughts. In the 1800s the French *enfant terrible*

Arthur Rimbaud (1854–1891) was advising us that becoming a poet involved a disordering of the senses. For him, excess was a creed and moderation a ticket to nowhere; it encouraged only staleness and mediocrity. Mind you, he gave up writing poetry before twenty and took a ticket to the wilds of Africa where he expired in his thirties. Fire in the belly is undeniably good, but beware the uncontrolled burn.

LIKE MOST OF the world I watched the Opening Ceremony of the Sydney 2000 Olympic Games, in which excess was the only possible vindication of a country's sporting obsession. As a classical music lover I was naturally impressed at the end when the flaming torch rose from the waters around Cathy Freeman to the strains of Berlioz's Te Deum (1849) — one of his truly excessive pieces, and one we were allowed to savour for longer than planned when the machinery stuck. But what gave me an even greater thrill was the music that accompanied the torch's final ascent to the top of the stadium; the big splashy tune at the end of **Percy Grainger's** (1882–1961) 'Imaginary Ballet' *The Warriors*, completed in 1916. It was an inspired choice: a piece about 'an orgy of war-like dances, processions and merry-making' by an Australian who was an athletic, outdoorsy type, running, hiking and cartwheeling through life. The music was as virile and over-the-top as the event it crowned. Grainger would have been delighted, I suspect. He would also have felt avenged; in 1956 it was suggested that Grainger write some music for the opening of the Olympic Games in Melbourne but the idea was dismissed as a joke. I was so pleased at this belated recognition of our greatest native-born musician that I rushed out to buy the CD soundtrack souvenir of the event when it was released just days later. Sadly, Grainger's music wasn't included.

There is a curious consistency in this exclusion, even all these years after his death in 1961. We still have trouble taking Percy Grainger seriously. Part of this is because he seems unimaginable as a real person; then again, such a bizarre personality could only have existed in reality. Nobody could have made him up. His excesses have such a tabloid tinge to them that he is one of the easiest composers to misrepresent. I probably do him no favours in the brief space of this book by including him in such a chapter, but it's hard to know just where else I could have slotted him in. **Lust**, perhaps (as he once wrote, 'I worship lust …'), but since he considered the exercise of that lust the supreme pleasure of his life, here he is. Was he — as his 1976 biographer John Bird contended — 'mad'? I have no idea. But one thing is for certain; he was mother's little boy.

RECIPE FOR UNUSUAL CHILDHOOD
(beginning in Melbourne, Australia, 1882)

Ingredients:
- 1 syphilitic, promiscuous alcoholic father
- 1 syphilitic (caught from husband), racially bigoted, over-protective mother with a predilection for the disciplinary horse-whip
- No siblings

Method: Try to blend the parents together in a typical late-Victorian marriage of convenience before having them realise some years and one child later that any combination is impossible. Place a statue of a Greek god at the foot of the bed during pregnancy in the hope that its remarkable qualities will magically transfer to the child. After birth, keep the child away from playmates his own age and instead fill his solitude with enforced piano lessons and practice. Add only a pinch (three months) of formal schooling. Avoid handling with the fingers, in fact, shun any physical contact for the first five years. After this, beat frequently with a whip.

Allow the twelve-year-old mix to rise away from home in the warm oven of a German conservatorium. Promote an unnatural interdependence by keeping mother and son together at all times, ensuring that the latter continues to be beaten regularly until the age of sixteen. Have mother maintain absolute control and power of veto over son's female contacts and prospective romantic interests. Continue in this way until son is almost forty.

Serve with lashings of ... well, serve with lashings period.

That Grainger turned out to be eccentric will hardly surprise after reading the above. Indeed, it is one of the 'nicest' adjectives we can use about him and it marries well with the often jolly and highly idiosyncratic arrangements he made of folksongs he and others collected in Britain and Scandinavia in the first quarter of the last century. Most of us know *Country Gardens* and the *Irish Tune from County Derry* (or as it is better known, *Danny Boy*) thanks to Grainger. Who wouldn't want to know a character with such endearing eccentricities?

- Grainger loved travelling by train, abjuring cars as much as possible after being involved in an accident. He always bought a second class ticket and slept sitting up.
- As he grew older, he liked to sleep at home under his piano.
- He gave up eating meat in 1924 but was not fond of vegetables. A favourite food was bread and jam, no butter.
- He disliked wearing hats over his peroxided hair and often looked so unkempt that he was twice arrested for vagrancy — once as he was traversing New York's Grand Central Station carrying a metal lamp.
- He lived in the same house in White Plains, New York, for forty years but only mowed his front lawn once.
- Rather than carry a briefcase, he would simply hang pens, pencils and other small items from his jacket on pieces of string.
- On some tours he preferred to hike from one engagement to another. While in South Africa in 1904 he

packed a knapsack after a concert in Pietermaritzburg and walked 65 miles to his next engagement in Durban, arriving at 6 pm the following evening. On another inter-city hike on that same tour he was escorted by a tribe of Zulu warriors whom he encountered en route.

- During a rehearsal of Grieg's Piano Concerto in the Sydney Town Hall in 1934, Grainger jumped down from the platform during an orchestral passage, sprinted down the aisle to the doors at the back of the hall and made it back to the piano in time for his cadenza.
- In 1932 he told a class at New York University that the three greatest composers were Bach, Delius and ... Duke Ellington.
- He loved wearing shirts made of brightly-coloured towelling.
- In 1928 he married his wife Ella at the end of a concert at the Hollywood Bowl before an amused audience of about 20,000. An orchestra of 126 played his work *To a Nordic Princess* (Ella was Swedish) and one of the witnesses to the ceremony was the film star Ramon Novarro. His new bride was unaware at the time that Grainger would be likely to bring out the whips during their honeymoon.

⚜

Grainger was an obsessive flagellant. He just loved his whips. The lash was his greatest sexual pleasure, and since he confessed even late in life that 'I hardly think of anything but sex', a nearby whip was an indispensable accessory. If an obliging woman was not around to take part, Grainger would happily whip himself. He documented many of his solo sessions with almost clinical precision, trying out various types of whip on himself and photographing the results. When he toured, his whips were packed in an extra bag for some recreation between concerts. In the early 1930s, he composed an exculpatory letter to be opened in the event of he or his wife Ella dying under the lash. The sound of whipcracks meshes rather strangely with the almost suburban strains of *Country Gardens*.

Since the Graingers married late it was always unlikely that they would have children. This is perhaps just as well, as Grainger freely admitted to having fantasies about whipping them, as well as committing incest with his daughters once they reached puberty. A resolute non-Christian, he at least made distinctions between good and evil when he declared his 'worship' of the latter. In his letters he veered constantly between self-condemnation and a defiant candour: 'I live for my lusts and I don't care if they kill me …' (1930). He had felt the same way since his early teens and even in middle-age regarded himself as a 'naughty' child who '… looks to be punished for it'. It sounds like just the sort of thing his mother would have said.

Rose Grainger was just a few days past her twenty-first birthday when she gave birth to Percy and kept her youthful looks as she matured. She and her son were often mistaken for brother and sister, or even husband and wife. Certainly no marriage could have been closer; the two were inseparable throughout their sojourns in Germany, London and the United States after leaving Melbourne in 1895. (Percy eventually took out U.S. citizenship.) Rose often accompanied her son on his tours as a pianist and was such a controlling presence in his romantic life that putative *amours* realised they were always going to get two for the price of one and eventually withdrew. It was no contest; Percy considered the relationship with his mother 'the only truly passionate love affair' of his life. The intimate tone of their letters to each other could easily be mistaken for that between lovers.

So it was perhaps understandable that rumours of incest began to circulate after the end of the First World War. They were untrue, but Rose — who was already in a highly fragile state of mind after several nervous breakdowns and the effects of her encroaching syphilis — quite literally tipped over the edge. In 1922 she committed suicide by jumping out of the eighteenth-floor window of a New York office building.

❦

The moral of the story: Grainger's childhood made him more than a little twisted. It also forged one of the truly original musical minds of the twentieth century. He felt his 'Australian-ness' keenly and was empowered by it to explore the fresh air outside the hothouse of European art music of the time. He gathered up folksongs like wild-flowers around Britain, Scandinavia and New Zealand and made countless arrangements of them, often with so-called 'elastic' scoring in which different combinations of instruments could be used according to circumstance. He experimented with complex rhythms and allowed players inside ensembles to wander off the common beat. He wrote for whistlers, harmoniums, ukuleles, musical glasses and big groups of 'tuneful' percussion instruments (some of which he invented). He tried to invent an electronic 'Free Music' that could ooze in any direction — just like the ripples of water fanning out from the boat that fascinated him on childhood sailing trips.

Grainger wrote that his life was '… one of kicking out into space while the world around me is dying of good taste'. This was obsession making a good point. We need the kickers and the hikers like Grainger. The whip does need to be cracked over our notions of 'good taste' that so often take us to a dead-end.

I sincerely hope that you feel emboldened to keep on sampling classical music after reading this book, but don't try to kid yourself that in doing so you have acquired 'good taste'. You should be delighted that you're sending your ears into new territory; but that's a different (and far more laudable) matter. 'Good taste' is a colourless antechamber to the vast carnival of things that are possible. Good music is certainly a passport to your own special place, but that place should be one with the windows open.

Grainger never wanted the energy of his music to be confused with jollity. In fact, he said the object of his work was not to entertain, but to 'agonise'. In making his obsessions both the fuel and substance of his oeuvre, Percy reminds us that good music is often about bad things.

In 1925 Grainger listed his ideal regime for the realisation of health and talent: '...give up all great hopes, all dislikes, all impatience, walk two to four hours daily, never smoke, never drink tea, coffee or alcohol, and always be in bed by 9.30 or 10 p.m.'

It's safe to say that **Leonard Bernstein** (1918–1990) never followed Grainger's advice. The former wonder-boy of American music — a brilliant twenty-five-year-old conducting debutant with the New York Philharmonic in 1943, a gifted pianist, composer of everything from symphonies to musicals, and ground-breaking music educator through his television specials and concerts — Bernstein's initial excess was one of energy. In conducting circles he was at first a dashing young buccaneer in among the aged and venerable; maestros were supposed to be the orchestras' tribal elders (we're still a little suspicious of conductors without a touch of grey). He turned the conductor into an action star, wielding his baton like a sword and launching himself into the air for the dramatic downbeats.

A story for the beautiful people: Bernstein was a starburst in the New York of the '40s and '50s. He was good-looking, charming, witty; the glamour-puss who whizzed up an after-show party by presiding at the piano in the company of scotch, cigarettes and other attractive young things. They loved him and he made every effort to repay them in kind. As a teenager Bernstein declared that he was going to 'try everything' in his lifetime.

Trying everything is a double-edged sword for those who seemingly have it all — especially talent. Some measure of success is guaranteed; enough to persuade that the right course has been found. And yet Bernstein was never entirely convinced: even as he excelled in one field, he began to rue his neglect of another. The paths of creator (composer) versus interpreter (conductor) were alternately the strongest lures; when he stepped down from the helm of the New York Philharmonic in 1969 after eleven seasons as Music Director he did so to concentrate on writing, but inevitably the temptation of the public's love drew him back to the podium.

The pendulum swung just as dramatically with his sexuality. Many eyebrows were raised when he married the actress Felicia Montealegre Cohn in 1951 — they had broken off their first engagement four years earlier. In 1976

Bernstein finally left his wife for another man, saying that 'I had to lead the rest of my life as I want.' When they tried to reconcile a year later it was too late: Felicia was dying from cancer.

After her death in 1978 Bernstein was haunted by guilt. He felt himself responsible for his wife's illness and remembered her prediction at the time of their break-up, '… you're going to die a bitter and lonely old man.' Certainly during the twelve years before his own death Bernstein behaved more and more like a sybaritic pasha, often trumpeting his own excesses (see the quote at the head of the chapter). In 1985 Bernstein said, '… the Will to Love guides my living from day to day, always has, and always has messed it up to a remarkable degree, and still does …'

The 'Love' that Bernstein cited was obviously a flexible concept to someone of his extraordinary intelligence. And whatever form it took, by day or night, Bernstein needed far too much of it. The Beautiful Young Thing turned Venerated (but outrageous) Old Man could never be satisfied.

Still, in 1957 he wrote that work of genius — *West Side Story*.

⚘

I actually met Bernstein in 1974. He was making his one trip to Australia on a tour with the New York Philharmonic. Tickets had been snapped up the moment his concerts were announced and by the time I tried to buy a seat all the concerts were sold out. My attempts to bribe friends or purchase a ticket from them at a hefty premium were unsuccessful. I was facing the prospect of missing Bernstein altogether.

As it turned out, the brazen confidence of a largely ignorant seventeen-year-old can be a powerful force. I resolved that if I couldn't see the Maestro in action I would at least let him know about this melancholy fact face-to-face.

I rang the Sydney Opera House (where he was appearing) and informed the Stage Door that I was an important broadcasting executive who was despatching a courier with some important documents for Bernstein to sign. Clutching a self-typed letter of entrée I duly presented myself at the end of the concert. Somehow I persuaded both the Opera House security and Bernstein's own retinue of my veracity and was ushered into his dressing room before the inevitable horde of admirers.

Bernstein had just showered and was reclining in his dressing gown, a chain-smoking odalisque. Nervously, I offered him my letter, to which Bernstein, showing greater perception than his helpers, responded: '… you read it.' It was a fairly pathetic 'I couldn't get in but I love your work' declaration, but Bernstein listened with far more attention than it deserved. At the end of my recital he jumped up from his couch. I noticed with surprise that he was shorter than me; even in repose, he seemed almost too big for the room, and I am rather on the diminutive side.

After a brief conversation he mentioned that it was his fifty-sixth birthday and the party was beginning forthwith.

The dressing room door swung open: sparkling wine and a cake were wheeled in on a trolley followed by the official party-goers, including the Australian Prime Minister, Gough Whitlam, and his wife. Bernstein introduced me to Mrs Whitlam as 'an old friend whom I've just met'. I recall having a long conversation with Bernstein's nineteen-year-old son, Alexander.

The night wore on. I decided I should ring my mother to inform her of the rather obvious news that I was running late.

'Where are you?' she asked.

'I'm in Leonard Bernstein's dressing room,' I replied, '… it's his birthday.'

'Well, you come home right now,' my mother said with some urgency.

Let's go to some more common garden excesses:

Niccolò Paganini (1782–1840) was a violinist of such unearthly talent and cadaverous appearance that it was said the Devil guided his bow. Paganini traded profitably on such gossip and spent the considerable proceeds on women and high stakes in gambling. When his depleted body began to go downhill in 1823, a doctor assumed the cause to be syphilis and prescribed massive doses of mercury and opium cigars. The mercury poisoned his system, loosening his teeth so much that he had to tie them together with twine in order to eat. Eventually all his lower teeth were extracted (without the benefit of anaesthetic; Paganini had to be held down during the procedure) and his ravaged jaw supported with a bandage. His public disdain for conventional morality and all the Devil talk had offended the hierarchy of the Church, who refused to allow the deceased virtuoso's burial in consecrated ground. Instead, his corpse was embalmed, dressed in performance garb and put in a coffin with a glass pane above its face. Paganini's son was later offered 30,000 francs to exhibit the cadaver in England.

The grog: Somehow you would expect this to go with the territory. Cirrhosis was a likely contributor to Beethoven's death (see **Anger**). Tchaikovsky admitted it was a problem. In fact it was a bit of a hoodoo for other Russian composers. **Modest Mussorgsky** (1839–1881) was a dreadful young sot who had been shaping up as one of the most original nineteenth century composers with his opera *Boris Godunov* (1869), the diabolic orchestral work *Night on Bare Mountain* (1867) (later to become one of the highlights of the Disney classic *Fantasia*), and the piano suite *Pictures at an Exhibition* (1874), now a staple of the orchestral repertoire in the orchestration by Ravel. His chronic alcoholism meant that he started many more works than he finished before his premature death at the age of forty-two — a human tragedy but an even bigger tragedy for music. The Irish-born **John Field** (1782–1837) was a great piano virtuoso and influential composer whose playing of his own Nocturnes captivated many a European salon and gave the young **Frederic Chopin** (1810–1849) more than a few ideas. Field spent a large part of his career in Russia and eventually made the bottle too much of a companion: in his forties he virtually stopped writing altogether and became known in certain circles as 'drunken John'. He asserted that the only reason he married one of his pupils was that she never paid for her lessons. The death of **Henry Purcell** (1659–1695) was said to have been caused by his wife's chagrin over the number of hours he spent at the local London tavern. She locked him out of the house, causing him to spend the night in the rain and precipitating his final illness.

Giacomo Puccini's two excesses were women and cigarettes. As you'll discover in **Anger**, his amorous exploits eventually paid a grim dividend. But so too did the smokes; the composer was diagnosed with inoperable throat cancer in 1924 and died while receiving X-ray treatment, leaving an unfinished opera, *Turandot*. In his lifetime Puccini's celebrity and good looks led him into many a temptation; while staying in a plush Vienna hotel his fag break was interrupted by the unexpected entrance of a naked woman into his suite. Puccini thought her mad and attempted to summon the hotel staff for aid, but on closer inspection of his visitor he decided that it was unwise to oppose the will of a lunatic. **Vincent Wallace** (1812–1865) permitted himself — somewhat illegally — an excess of wives, contriving to be married to an Irish woman and an American at the same time. Perhaps he was confused by the frequent travelling occasioned by a restless spirit and a near-Wagnerian capacity for incurring debt. Wallace's itinerary included a stint in Australia during the 1830s. An outstanding pianist and violinist (he was dubbed the 'Australian Paganini'), he founded a music academy in Sydney and lived for a while at the Bush Inn in Hobart, where it is said he wrote much of what became the smash hit opera *Maritana*, first performed in London in 1845.

We've already touched upon the propensity to violence as demonstrated by aristocrat/composer **Don Carlo Gesualdo** (see **Lust**). Being a man of means, he employed ten young men to beat him three times a day. It is said that during these sessions he was 'wont to smile joyfully'. I am relieved to report that **Johannes Brahms** (1833–1897) has been cleared of a century-old charge of excessive cruelty to animals. Scandal-mongers put it about that Brahms would spear cats with arrows from his apartment window in Vienna, reel them up like trout, and transcribe their dying mews into chamber music. It is now thought that these accusations of felicide were a red herring propagated by Wagner, who was arguably rather too close to his dogs.

<hr>

So much for the destructive excesses. These are more innocent:

Sergey Prokofiev (1891–1953) was once evicted from his apartment for playing the same piano chord 218 times. A tally was kept by the downstairs tenant.

Anton Bruckner (1824–1896), the pious and

unworldly Austrian organist and composer, developed a condition called numeromania that compelled him to count everything — cathedral gables, stars, leaves on trees; even the number of bars in his lengthy symphonies. Orchestral musicians struggling through a less than inspiring performance of Bruckner have been known to do the same — it helps to pass the time.

Erik Satie (1866–1925), whose static *Three Gymnopédies* for piano (1888) still sound as fresh as the day they were written, practised a defiant eccentricity that positioned him as an official laughing-stock for much of his career. His ballet *Relâche* (1924) had trouble pulling a crowd, possibly because the title translates from the French as 'this performance is cancelled'. In fact, Satie was a master of the eye-catching title appended to very short piano works — *Three Pieces in the Shape of a Pear* (1903), *Desiccated Embryos* (1913), *Bureaucratic Sonatina* (1917) — the list goes on. His invention of so-called 'Furniture Music' is a precursor to today's Muzak — but we won't hold that against him. He lived most of his life in a drab Parisian suburb, renting the same room for nearly thirty years; not even the concierge was allowed in. He drank excessively (a legacy of his earlier cabaret-hopping life in Montmartre) but lived frugally, save for a couple of obsessive indulgences — seven identical velvet suits, consituting his entire wardrobe, plus a collection of umbrellas.

Giacomo Rossini (1792–1868) could either go like a chainsaw or barely leave his bed. Sometimes he could do both at the same time. There's a story that had him churning out the pages on a lazy day between the sheets.

A page slipped to the floor, and rather than leaving his cocoon to pick it up, Rossini simply wrote out a new one. The sheer speed and facility this suggests was no musical urban myth; he wrote *The Barber of Seville* (1816) in less than a fortnight (albeit with a bit of recycling here and there) and suggested that the best incentive to work was to 'wait until the evening before opening night'. Even this deadline was too loose for Rossini at times. The overture to his opera *The Thieving Magpie* (1817) was written on the very day of the work's premiere, with Rossini locked in a room by stage-hands who collected the sheets of newly-inscribed manu-script as they came sailing out through a window.

These brief periods of slavery paid off handsomely for Rossini. He was world-famous in his early twenties and col-lected the cash to match. Of all the composers in this book, he was probably the wealthiest, building homes in several European cities and hosting celebrated salons in later life. Paying for his next meal was not a problem when he elected to retire at the age of thirty-seven, which was just as well, because he loved his food and even lent his creativity to cuisine, inventing the dish 'Tournedos Rossini'. To have written the sparkling, witty music that the world still loves — a recording of Rossini overtures will always add champagne to your collection — to have been a famous dispenser of *bon mots*, to have become the most famous composer in the world and then opted for an early and opulent retirement; all this would suggest a contented life. Not so, for Rossini was prey to such severe depression that contemporary writers have suggested he suffered from a bipolar disorder (manic-depressive illness). Mood swings, money, talent, celebrity — all put to marvellous purpose, but almost too much for a single life. The second half of Rossini's life (his 'retirement') lasted longer than the first and he soldiered on as a living legend into his late seventies.

⟨※⟩

Big opera: Motorists who gasp in wonder at Australian roadside apparitions like The Big Banana were born 350 years too late to savour the gigantism of **Antonio Cesti's** (1623–1669) opera *The Golden Apple*. Cesti veered from the sacred to the secular in his lifestyle, being both a Franciscan monk and an operatic tenor in his native Italy before his burgeoning stage career and habit of dropping the habit when in the company of sopranos forced an exit from the monastery after his superiors excoriated his 'dishonourable and irregular life'. We don't know what he looked like but his personality was obviously one that irritated his competitors in the music world to the point that his early death was attributed to poison (being a composer was dangerous in the seventeenth century).

One hopes Cesti didn't succumb to bad fruit. It would have been an irony given the success of his huge *Apple* staged at the Viennese royal court in 1668. It was by far the most costly opera of its time, requiring twenty-four complete sets depicting everything from the underworld to the home of the gods. In between there were forests, flying dragons, storms at sea and people descending from clouds, all in a new theatre purpose-built for the performances in a Baroque cross between Wagner's Bayreuth and Las Vegas. Cesti had warmed up for this epic by composing an equestrian ballet the year before.

But when one talks about 'big opera' the popular favourite is Verdi's *Aida*, first performed at the Cairo Opera House in 1871 and obligingly set in ancient Egypt. The exotic locale gives the cue for ambitious producers to dig deep for the decor, particularly in open-air performances which seem to suit this opera so well. You can have it all; virtual pyramids, a Sphinx or two, a chorus of Egyptians stretching to the horizon and the cavalcade of horses and elephants whose on-stage critiques of the show have littered much theatrical legend and left many skid-marks. It's said that Noël Coward sat through a production that featured both an incontinent elephant and a less than satisfactory soprano in the lead; he later remarked that the night would have been improved by shoving the singer's head up the animal's backside.

The French called the genre *grand opéra* and the genre certainly spent much of the nineteenth century on this elephantine scale. King of the heap — the nineteenth-century version of Andrew Lloyd Webber — was **Giacomo Meyerbeer** (1791–1864), whose colossal operas became tourist attractions. Audiences loved the action in the crowd scenes (the more violent the better) and the special effects. We haven't changed really. Meyerbeer operas always have hordes of soldiers, peasants and monks. The soldiers try to kill the peasants and the monks try to mediate, resulting in their own deaths. Much blood is spilt over timpani rolls and roaring brass but not a drop touches the orchestra. The Huguenots in his 1836 opera are massacred by the Catholics in sixteenth-century Paris, sinful nuns are raised from the dead for a bacchanale in *Robert the Devil* (1831), and Vasco da Gama's entire crew are massacred aboard ship during a storm at sea in *The African Woman* (1865). Even too much is never enough: the entire cast is wiped out in an explosion at the end of *The Prophet* (1849). With an outcome like that I'd be looking for a better prophet.

Of course, with **Richard Wagner** (1813–1883) and his *Ring* cycle these explosions are mere penny crackers in the fireworks of existence. He wrote about nothing less than all-out apocalypse (see **Triumph**).

<hr />

When too much is barely enough: There have been few composers as prolific as **Georg Philipp Telemann** (1681–1767). He wrote thousands of works, achieving all this from a standing start, given that he was almost completely self-taught.

Telemann's first wife, a lady-in-waiting, died in childbirth fifteen months after their wedding. His second wife, the daughter of a Frankfurt council clerk, was made of sterner stuff: she produced eight sons and two daughters. It would seem that she was more than a match for her husband's prodigious energy. While he took time out from reproductive duties to pen another one of his 1400-odd cantatas or 125 or so concertos (to name a few), Mrs Telemann took up with a Swedish officer and eventually fled Hamburg in the company of her new man, leaving her husband with massive debt. The scandal was the talk of the town and became the subject of a satirical play that was banned by the authorities. Poor cuckolded Telemann applied a grim humour to his situation, appealing for financial aid from friends with a letter that began: 'My lot is now much easier to bear, Extravagance departed with my spouse.'

Excess is in the ear of the beholder: A final word from Mozart on the subject. After a rehearsal of his new opera *The Abduction from the Seraglio* in 1781, the Austrian Emperor Joseph II bailed up the composer with the comment that there were 'too many notes'. The confident twenty-five-year-old replied that there were exactly as many notes as required. In the end, who can really judge how much is too much? Then again, lucky Mozart never watched Jerry Springer.

One can easily become obsessed with these flaws and distortions in composers' personalities and I see that this part of the book has run to excessive length. Are such life details irrelevant to the main game of the music itself? For me, they simply underline the miracle of the music's existence. Life is a matter of jostling through, saying 'excuse me' and collecting a frequent kick in the kidneys while trying to maintain an air of grace in the throng. Music also has to bump and grind its way to the cruel air of the outside world. People create because, in the end, they just can't help themselves, but being creatures of remarkable imagination they construct barricades with their idiosyncrasies to impede the work's passage. Maybe Father Bach had the balance right. Since his only excess was that of children (itself a healthy sign) he wrote fluidly and voluminously for all his life (see **Hope**).

In the delicate matter of Love, obsession nurtures expectations. It imagining they have been fulfilled, we feel the rush of conquest, of all-out triumph. Suitably inflated, we press on further into the affair.

⇢ TRIUMPH ⇠

"The whole will become … the greatest work of poetry ever written."

RICHARD WAGNER about his *Ring* cycle

It is one of life's pettiest — and greatest — satisfactions: to be proven right.

In CHARLIE CHAPLIN'S autobiography there is a story of an early dramatic encounter with classical music. In 1913, while still an unknown stage comedian touring the United States with an English vaudeville troupe, the twenty-four-year-old took a few days off from the grind of provincial shows to make a solo trip to New York. This oasis of comparative luxury included a good hotel, half a bottle of champagne and a first time visit to the opera; Wagner's *Tannhäuser* (1845) at the Metropolitan. Chaplin knew neither German nor anything about the opera's plot. Yet when the Pilgrim's Chorus began in Act Three, the future Little

Tramp found himself weeping uncontrollably. 'What people sitting next to me must have thought I don't know,' he wrote. '[The music] seemed to sum up all the travail of my life.' World celebrity for Chaplin as a film comedian was only a few months away.

Whether or not Chaplin sensed a kindred spirit, he was to return to Wagner much later in his film *The Great Dictator*, a daring spoof on Hitler released at the beginning of the Second World War. Perhaps he knew of Hitler's Wagnerian passion. But there it is; when the dictator dreams of world domination he performs a balloon dance with the globe to the ethereal strains of Wagner's Act One Prelude to *Lohengrin* (1850). What a strange trio of control freaks; the actor, the demented autocrat and the composer. In his own way each wished to manufacture a complete and detailed world running on its own rules, while insisting we all come along for the ride. Chaplin's was the world of the past. Wagner and Hitler saw themselves as emissaries of the future.

<hr />

There are two good reasons for not including Richard Wagner in our *Swooning* collection. The most obvious is that more words have been written about Wagner than about any other figure in musical history. He also leads the field as the recipient of more spleen, more hyperbole, more imitation and more analysis (mind you, he gave as good as he got). How is it possible to say more?

The second; well, this modest tome is an attempt to relate states of mind and emotion experienced by some of history's great composers to those we experience today so that we can compare our responses with theirs and follow — or avoid — their example. Composers are like us, in other words. This is an implausible claim in the case of Wagner. He was definitely not normal, and of all the composers he is the one who can make the listener feel most insignificant. There is virtually nothing in his life, behaviour or achievement that suggests the everyday. His charm could completely seduce women from the nearby arms of their husbands. His temper was frightening and easily inflamed. His grief over the death of the household dog was debilitating (possibly his most human trait). And his self-belief enabled him to triumph against every setback in the book: poverty, indifference, hostility, exile and subterfuge. Long after any mortal would have given up, Wagner kept faith in himself and his work, sustained by the credo that he was the greatest musician in the world. He was the Muhammad Ali of nineteenth-century music — possibly of all music. His father-in-law (and biggest fan) Franz Liszt said, '… in the matter of glory Wagner fasted for thirty years.' In his sixties, that fast broke; Wagner was proved right. He had triumphed.

When our confidence in ourselves and our ideas suffers a series of painful low blows it takes a sturdy constitution not to be deflected from long-term goals. Wagner's absence of doubt would almost be classified as that of a megalomaniac were it not for the fact that he actually fulfilled his intentions and persevered for as long as it took: the *Ring* cycle, for instance, occupied twenty-eight years from conception to first complete performance (1848–1876) — in a new theatre custom-built for the event according to the composer's specifications, of course — during which time Wagner had revolutionised Western music with his *Tristan and Isolde*. The quote at the head of this chapter doesn't seem so outlandish, after all. The *Ring* is certainly one of the most *influential* works of poetry ever written, and that has to account for something. But what sort of person could make such a claim on their own behalf in the first place?

Not a particularly pleasant one — but being merely 'pleasant' was never his intention. That was part of the make-up of Mr Average. 'I am not made like other people,' he insisted, '… the world owes me what I need.' In the end the world gave it to him, but only after a lifetime of asking. Nobody ever demanded charity with such self-assurance. Imagine a letter arriving out of the blue from a comparative stranger saying something like 'Give us a few quid, would you? I'm knocking out the greatest poem ever written. Do you have a spare bed for a couple of months? You'll find my company irresistible. Congratulations — I don't offer these privileges to just anyone.' In a nutshell, this was a typical Wagner *spiel*. You'd be careful about saying yes, I suspect. Some did and lived to regret it.

Wagner was born in Leipzig, Germany, in 1813. His father died when Wagner was six months old. His mother had been friendly with a local actor and married him only nine months after being widowed. Many have suggested that the actor, Ludwig Geyer, was Wagner's biological father after all: Wagner Senior was a police chief.

When your teenager suddenly declares a life ambition that bears no relation to their sphere of knowledge, don't laugh. Little Richard (he was short) decided to become a composer at the age of fifteen after hearing Beethoven's Ninth Symphony. I love it when people experience a revelatory thunderbolt and thereafter behave as if fired out of a gun. But Wagner was a non-performer at school and completely untrained in music; he might as well have said that he was going to walk to the moon. Even with such dedicated zeal his musical studies were sketchy at best (see **Some Musical Life Tips**). He could only pick at the piano, played no other instrument, and was a so-so score reader. Somehow, it didn't matter. Wagner took what he needed and allowed gut instinct to refine the rest. Still fifteen, he wrote a play called *Leubald,* modelled after Shakespearean tragedy, that killed off so many of the large cast they had to be brought back as ghosts in order to speak the final lines. Fortunately, maturity never taught him greater restraint.

Wagner drank and gambled his way through an incomplete university course and wrote bad music that had audiences in hysterics. Hardly a propitious start to classical music's most controversial career. And then it started: words and music (he was always his own librettist) for operas that quickly evolved into an art-form that he termed 'music drama'. The distinctions between the two you can read elsewhere, especially in Wagner's own voluminous writings which reveal him to be something of a futurist and a racist; his views on Judaism met with Hitler's approval a hundred years later and (until recently) saw his music boycotted in Israel.

<hr />

This guy was trouble. He secured a job as a musical director in a small German town called Magdeburg in 1834 and began a pattern of incurring enormous debts and then doing a runner when the creditors came calling. Wagner spent money all his life like there was no tomorrow. He wrote, 'I can't live on a miserable pittance!'; to which others would have responded, 'Who does he think he is ... a genius?' Well — yes.

He fell in love with an actress called Minna Planer and married her in 1836. She had been led astray at fifteen by an army captain and had an illegitimate daughter. Six months after marrying Wagner she decamped with a businessman. They were eventually reunited and Minna had to endure Wagner's subsequent jealousy even as he pursued his own affairs. After an escape from one bankruptcy too many the pair snuck off to Paris in 1839 and lived like paupers for the next two-and-a-half years. Wagner was reduced to making piano arrangements of musical trash to put some bread on the table; he even suffered a spell in a debtors' prison.

But instead of jumping out the nearest window or even admitting that it was time to consider some other way to make a living, he completed *The Flying Dutchman* (1843), a sort of seafaring ghost story about redemption through love — a favourite subject of Wagner's. Listen to the Overture from this opera as it presents an astonishing example of just where he was going in his music — a storm at sea, the wind howling in the rigging, the crash of the waves against the hull. But the music isn't just picture painting; there is an elemental quality about it. This is no mere representation of nature. It *is* a force of nature (fellow composer **Charles Gounod** (1818–1893) called it 'a hurricane'), charged with a 'take no prisoners' attitude that rampages through his subsequent work.

For sheer sonic impact Wagner is like going to a rock concert. 'Listening' is too passive a response; instead, one has to submit. Charm has nothing to do with it. An audience just has to decide whether or not it wants to be slapped around until it likes the sensation. Many didn't, of course. The printed vitriol that was poured upon Wagner's work from the 1840s would fill several entertaining volumes by itself. It also makes you wonder how anybody these days would survive such constant bucketing.

WAGNER: THE CRITICS RAVED!!

*"… inspired by the riots of cats scampering around
an ironmonger's shop in the dark."*
Alexandre Dumas père

*"… an old Italian painting of a martyr whose
intestines are slowly unwound from his body
on a reel."*
Eduard Hanslick

"… a sort of chromatic moan."
Hector Berlioz

*"… an endlessly ruminating monster afflicted with
a revolting eructation."*
Ludwig Spiedel

*"… affected, sapless, soulless, beginningless,
endless, topless, bottomless, topsy-turviest,
tongs-and-boniest doggerel …"*
John Ruskin

"Wagner's art is diseased."
Friedrich Nietzsche

… there is so much more.

Beware the smart man who asks for money:
Fortunately, Wagner also had his supporters and they sometimes responded in spectacular fashion to his frequent calls
for assistance. The dénouements from some of these situations show the dangers inherent in extending charity to
genius …

1. **FAVOUR:** Franz Liszt, the mid-nineteenth-century
   Power Man of music, championed Wagner in print and
   performance, conducting the premiere of *Lohengrin* in
   1850.
   GRATITUDE: Wagner, only two years Liszt's junior,
   responded by becoming his son-in-law after fathering
   three children by Liszt's daughter, Cosima, while she was
   inconveniently married to someone else.

2. **FAVOUR:** Otto Wesendonck, wealthy silk merchant,
   lent Wagner money during the 1850s and allowed him
   to live on one of his Swiss estates at a vastly reduced rent.
   GRATITUDE: Wagner conducted a long and passionate affair with Wesendonck's wife Mathilde. The
   interception of their love letters by Wagner's wife in
   1858 precipitated the final rupture in the composer's
   own marriage. (She had endured numerous other affairs
   of Wagner's; in 1850, he almost eloped to the Orient
   with another young admirer.) The musical fallout of the
   Wesendonck episode resulted in perhaps the most influential opera ever composed, *Tristan and Isolde* (all about
   love, of course). You could say it was the adultery we had

to have. When Mr Wesendonck tactfully purchased some of Wagner's manuscripts, enabling the composer to 'move on', Wagner went to Paris and set himself up in high style, employing a servant and a valet, and paying the high rent three years in advance. The money disappeared very quickly.

3. **FAVOUR:** In 1864 the teenage, gay, and incipiently mad King Ludwig II of Bavaria responded to Wagner's printed appeal for financial aid by giving him carte blanche to produce his works in Munich and an almost unlimited supply of funds for living expenses. The first big event to come from this was the premiere of *Tristan and Isolde* in 1865, conducted by Hans von Bülow.

GRATITUDE: Wagner went overboard with extravagance. His spell over the adoring King aroused the opposition of the court and he was pressured into leaving Munich in 1865. Still clutching the King's gift of an open chequebook, Wagner installed himself at a palatial estate on Lake Lucerne, spending everyone else's money (in Wagnerese, his due worth) on necessary opulence: silks, furs, perfumes, wallpaper of yellow leather traced in gold or violet velvet, orientalia and immaculate gardens. As he said, 'I must have brilliance and beauty and light.' Oh, yes: in return for Maestro Bülow's worshipful service on the podium, Wagner took Mrs Bülow as his mistress (see 1). Ludwig eventually went completely insane and drowned himself in 1886.

What is remarkable about all the exploited donors listed above is the extent of their magnanimity. Bülow, while the subject of international humiliation over his repeated cuckolding, almost congratulated his estranged wife on her involvement with a higher order of being. Wagner's acolytes believed in him with the sort of fervour we associate these days with religious cults. And in a sense, this *was* a religion; the new religion of Art. All that remained was to build a home temple, a shrine to Wagner's art and the natural dwelling place of Wagner's immense cycle *The Ring of the Nibelung*, completed in 1874; a fifteen-hour epic in instalments that takes four nights to perform. And incredibly, this was achieved in the German town of Bayreuth by 1876, thanks to help from subscriptions, Wagner's concert fees and a generous handout from the white knight King. The so-called Festival Theatre is the architectural incarnation of Wagner's ideas about 'music-drama' and theatre design. It is still one of the acoustic marvels of the world, with a hooded pit masking the huge orchestra from the audience's sightline while deflecting the sound onto the vast stage. Even in the twenty-first century, going to a Bayreuth Festival is still the supreme experience for thousands of artistic pilgrims.

Want to stick around? Start a dynasty: live long and breed late — this appears to be the reproductive credo of the Wagner clan. Consider this: Wagner was born in 1813. His only son, Siegfried (named after the hero of the *Ring* cycle then being written — Life imitating Art), was born in 1869 when Richard was fifty-six. Wagner Senior died in early 1883 in his seventieth year and Siegfried was inexorably drawn into the family musical tradition after studies in architecture and travels through India and China. I do feel more than a tinge of sympathy for Siegfried Wagner, named after an operatic hero and the only son of such an extraordinary father; it might have been safer to stay in the Orient designing pagodas. Cosima — Richard's widow — survived him by nearly fifty years; she died in 1930. Siegfried was married in 1915 to an Englishwoman, Winifred, who was nearly thirty years his junior. A formidable personality, more Wagnerian than her husband, she pursued an ill-advised friendship with Hitler who was one of the biggest Wagner groupies. Winifred survived her husband by another fifty years, right through to 1980 — nearly one hundred years after the death of her father-in-law.

Siegfried and Winifred's two sons, Wieland and Wolfgang, both made their careers in the family 'business' by taking over the Bayreuth Festival after the Second World War and mounting innovative productions of their grandfather's works. Wieland died in 1966 but Wolfgang has clung tenaciously to the artistic reins of the Wagner shrine at the beginning of the twenty-first century. And there are plenty more Wagners to come; in fact, the clan has been fighting publicly over the line of succession and control, much like the squabbling of gods, giants and gnomes over power and gold in the *Ring* cycle. And we know what happened to *them*.

⬦

Music's other triumphant career belongs to Wagner's contemporary, **Giuseppe Verdi** (1813–1901). One hundred years after his death, he is still the most-performed opera composer in the world, and the company that is brave enough not to include some Verdi in their annual season will have a hard time at the box-office. His is the ultimate operatic list of hits, including *Rigoletto* (1851), *La traviata* (1853), *Il trovatore* (1853), *Aida* (1871) and *Otello* (1887).

But **when talent comes knocking at the door, it is often sent packing**. When the talented teenage Verdi arrived from the provinces to audition for the prestigious Milan Conservatory in 1832, he was rejected. According to the authorities (none of whose names we remember), Giuseppe was a foreigner, too old, and played the piano with his hands in an 'incorrect' position. The composer never learned of these reasons in his lifetime. Years later, this same institution asked Verdi for permission to be named after him; he was not amused by the gall of a club wanting to adopt the title of someone they didn't want as a member (to misquote Groucho Marx). 'They didn't want me young. They cannot have me old,' he said.

Verdi's unfortunate brush with authority certainly strikes a personal chord. While lacking his talent I had nevertheless auditioned successfully for admittance to a conservatorium high school at the age of eleven. Four years later I was shown the door when it was considered that my own keyboard prowess was not up to standard. This caused some commotion around the place because I had topped the class in music theory, but the authorities were unacquainted with the notion that a career in music could be pursued without being able to play the piano. (Berlioz and Wagner managed quite well, as we've seen.) When my exam results came through in non-musical subjects, they were sufficiently impressive for me to be awarded a Commonwealth Scholarship and a Senior Secondary Bursary. The one complication, of course, was that I had been expelled. This caused the school authorities to reconsider and I was asked back. Too late. To have been deemed unworthy in front of classmates and peers had shot a hole in my self-esteem; I declined the conservatorium's latest invitation. So ended my formal education — I was fifteen. To this day I have no qualifications to speak of except an Honorary Doctorate kindly awarded to me by the University of Central Queensland for my work in broadcasting. When my alma mater recently held a gala affair to celebrate its most illustrious alumni, I was asked to be a Master of Ceremonies; a sort of re-entry into Wagner's Valhalla via the tradesmen's entrance. Being less capable than Verdi of holding a grudge,

I accepted the engagement while reminding the Director that I would be appearing under false pretences. One of these days I must get back to the piano.

⁕

Back to Verdi's more impressive fightback story. In the late 1830s the young composer was happily married with two young children, a girl and a boy. He was struggling to make his way — having secured a good private musical education after his Conservatory rejection — with the promise of an opera to be staged at Milan's La Scala. Then, catastrophe — within the space of two years Verdi lost his entire family to illness. When his wife completed this sad trio of deaths in June 1840 the composer was in the throes of writing (of all things) a comedy called *Un giorno di regno* (King for a Day). Under these circumstances one can only begin to imagine Verdi's enthusiasm for humour, so it is understandable that the premiere was a disaster and the opera was withdrawn as soon as the curtain came down to shouts of derision.

The shattered composer vowed never to write music again and became a virtual recluse, taking his meals occasionally at a nearby trattoria. Now follows one of classical music's most famous stories …

Verdi literally bumped into the Director of La Scala in the street during a solitary walk on a winter evening, the snow falling thickly. The Director, Signor Merelli, dragged the reluctant composer aside and forced on him a libretto for his consideration. On returning to his lodgings, Verdi says he threw the manuscript onto the table 'with a violent gesture'. It fell open at the line '*Va, pensiero, sull'ali dorate*' (Fly, thought, on golden wings) sung by the captive Hebrew slaves in ancient Babylon under the reign of Nebuchadnezzar. That was it; inspiration burst into life, and Verdi became instantly famous when his completed *Nabucco* opened in 1842. He never looked back and died a national hero nearly sixty years later. '*Va, pensiero*' is still his most famous melody.

⁂

The Frenchman **Georges Bizet** (1838–1875) once said that 'Wagner is Verdi with the addition of style'. Ouch — then again, the greatest invective heaped upon composers has come from their peers. Bizet himself was killed by indifference, some say, when his masterpiece *Carmen* opened to a glacial reception and an overwhelmingly hostile press in March 1875. He had taken the genre of opéra-comique, which interspersed singing with dialogue and was considered a vehicle for funny and satirical subjects, and turned it into a story of seduction and sexual jealousy set in sunny Spain; Carmen herself is stabbed to death at the end by her spurned and demented lover at a bullfight. The audience, not receiving their expected jolly night out, sat on their hands. Bizet paced the street outside the theatre saying, '…this time I am really sunk.'

Depression paved the way for illness and the composer passed away the following June as *Carmen* continued to play to half-empty houses; he was thirty-six. If only … if only; four months later a triumphant production in Vienna started the opera on its way around the world. Perhaps I should write The Opera, because it is up there with Puccini's *La bohème* as the genre's number 1 hit. *Carmen* was Tchaikovsky's favourite opera, and the philosopher (and former Wagner acolyte) Nietzsche hailed the work as a sort of clarifying Wagnerian antidote. All too late for its composer …

In 1905 **Maurice Ravel** (1875–1937) was considered by many to be one of France's most talented composers — except the eminent judges of the Prix de Rome at the Paris Conservatoire, where Ravel studied on and off for fourteen years. This competition for composers was considered highly prestigious and the First Prize included a stint of completely subsidised residence in the Eternal City; previous winners had included Berlioz, Bizet and Debussy. Ravel had flunked out in his three previous attempts and the 1905 entry would be his last, as he had hit the age limit of thirty. But it seems he had never been your standard academic's sort of guy (what *is* it about conservatoria?) and this time Ravel was knocked out in the preliminary round. Scandal! Parisian musical society was outraged and the controversy could only be quelled by the resignation of the Conservatoire's Director. Ravel went sailing with friends in Holland. Somebody somewhere might recall the names of the Conservatoire judges in 1905 but most people know who wrote *Bolero*.

⸻

'The Brat Johann': For our final view of triumph we go to the traditional family battleground of father versus son — in this case, the Strauss Affair. Take two Johanns in old Vienna: father (I, born 1804) and son (II, born 1825). Father made a success by fanning the new dance craze, the waltz, and playing his own compositions with his own orchestra. Johann Senior also sired a total of thirteen children; fortunately, six of these were with his wife (he had a second, larger family of love-children with his mistress). It was common enough for a non-musical father to disapprove of a son's artistic leanings for fear that the life of a musician was not only impecunious, but also slightly disreputable. The elder Johann — although a successful musician — felt much the same way and tried to steer his first-born into a career as a banker. The Strauss genes would not be so easily suppressed and young Johann dropped his bookkeeping studies in 1842 in favour of music. His father immediately detected the prospect of a competitor in the family ('... the brat Johann also intends to write waltzes although he has not got a clue about them ...') but was powerless to halt the surge of public interest in the emergence of another Kapellmeister Strauss. The young Johann's debut at Dommayer's Casino in October 1844 was an immediate success. Johann I died in 1849, having made a big musical career from humble origins in the suburbs of Vienna. But it was the son he tried to keep away from a professional music life who dominated European light music for the second half of the nineteenth century, who wrote the immortal *Blue Danube* waltz (1867) and was eventually dubbed 'The Waltz King'.

Ah — the spoils of victory. When all has capitulated in your favour in music or love there comes a chapter where one can settle back to drink and savour some heady wine.

⟶ JOY ⟵

"Great art can be happy as well as tragic … the
time for any serious effort is past …"
EMMANUEL CHABRIER

Music should exist only when it is absolutely necessary not to have silence. When you've heard as
much music as I have over forty years, however, the
restless mind becomes an endless storehouse of re-
collected sound. I find the mental jukebox really
fires up on long walks in remote places. It's a
dreadful habit when one should be opening the
ears to nature's symphony: wind, bird song, distant
running water. Instead — and no doubt prompted
by the rhythm of one's tramping feet — I launch
into a medley of Western Art Music's Top 300.
Slow movements don't match my mood; I pour my
exhilaration into a spontaneous mental soundtrack
that acquires more trombones, crashing cymbals
and speed with each successive hilltop.

I TOOK A sabbatical in 1999 and went to live for a couple of months in a small town in southern France. After a while I managed to look as indolent as the rest of its seemingly unemployed populace. Long days could be wasted in the contemplation of a well-written paragraph over a demi-litre of anything intoxicating. On days when I wanted to feel 'productive', opening up the windows of a former self to release the stale odours of a Protestant work ethic, I would take a track that wound precipitously behind the village into what was called the Sea of Rock. A couple of bends later all trace of living civilisation was erased, giving way to overgrown tracks, limestone outcrops and long-abandoned stone farmhouses battered to ruins by encroaching scrub.

This particular morning I decided to keep going on to the next town, a good ten kilometres away. The path ran along the top of a nearby escarpment, necessitating a long climb. The day was glorious and the composers kept me wonderful company as I ascended. When I reached the highest point of the walk I stood dangerously close to a cliff edge, fanned by the wind, looking at the distant Cévennes mountains. I felt actively happy, exultant. And whose music surged through my cerebellum to fit the moment? Monsieur Emmanuel Chabrier.

The association of Chabrier's music with high altitudes is very appropriate. He was a mountain man, born in the Auvergne region of France in 1841. Perhaps as a child he heard some of the folksongs of the area that would become so famous in Joseph Canteloube's orchestral arrangements nearly a hundred years later.

Chabrier was a musically gifted child, but as the son of a lawyer these proclivities were considered frivolous and he dutifully studied law, graduating in 1861 and taking a job in the French Ministry of the Interior. He remained a government employee for nearly twenty years.

There are valuable lessons for us in Chabrier's life and art: **There is as much profundity in laughter as in tragedy:** 'Stop laughing — this is serious!' is a phrase I remember from orchestral rehearsals back in my days as a music student. We've all been persuaded that the deep and meaningful belongs to drama and a furrowed brow. When Chabrier moved to Paris from the provinces in 1856, the City of Light was the home of grand opera at its Grandest; personal tragedies in historic settings with big sets, big choruses, impossible love, betrayal and death. This was the meat of art; comedies were the dessert, and therefore of less consequence.

Chabrier found this intolerable. 'Art with a capital letter, serious Art, is bogged down and stagnating', he wrote to a friend. Why was a frown more important? He was drawn to comedy. In his early twenties, fresh out of law school, he started two operettas with his friend, the poet Paul Verlaine. In the 1870s he completed two 'light' stage works: *L'Étoile* (1877) (something of a masterpiece) and *Une Éducation manquée* (1879). One of his few orchestral works, the *Joyous March* (1888), had the orchestra in stitches during its first rehearsal. This wasn't laughter of derision; they had simply tuned in to its sheer exuberance. Chabrier's most-performed piece is his orchestral rhapsody *España* (1883), a souvenir of a recent holiday with his family on the Iberian peninsula during which the composer confessed in ribald fashion to a fascination with women's swimwear. One can imagine his eyeballs popping out on those Spanish beaches. *España* almost explodes from the orchestra in good performance. No mere frippery in Chabrier's earthy comedy — the music has what they call 'grunt'. The composer **Vincent d'Indy** (1851–1931) called him 'the angel of drollery'.

What does this mean? Chabrier tells us that life's vicissitudes can be laughed at and wept over. Both responses bear witness to its truth but one of them is definitely more fun. What Leonard Bernstein called 'the joy of music' was Chabrier's artistic and philosophic credo. For the self-titled 'clog-dancing Auvergnat' (a reference to his unpretentious country origins), music was the earth under our feet, the curve of a woman waist-deep in water, the colours of a painting by one of his Impressionist friends, attacking the ivories with gusto — he was famed as 'a slayer of pianos' — and a good rollicking dance as the spice in a too-short life. This was true in Chabrier's case; syphilis took him at only fifty-three and the formerly boisterous composer eventually conceded that not even his Muse could arrest his decline. He wrote: '… poor dear music, my poor dear friend, so you no longer want me to be happy? I love you though, and I rather think you'll be the death of me.'

Trust your mid-life crisis — it's telling you something: In 1880, Chabrier was thirty-nine, a respectable public servant in the Ministry of the Interior, happily married with two sons, a perfect picture of nine-to-five bourgeois respectability. True, he consorted with artsy friends, knocked out loud piano music at parties and dabbled with comic operas, but since he'd never attended a music conservatory these were considered merely amateur pursuits.

In that same year Chabrier was taken to Munich by friends to hear Wagner's *Tristan and Isolde*. The experience proved cathartic. Chabrier was sobbing just minutes into the Prelude. Some hurried examination of his life's purpose must have followed. The results were dramatic; two months short of his fortieth birthday, he gave up a completely secure job, let what was left of his hair down and took the plunge into the financially uncertain puddle of freelance composition.

His immediate circle were concerned for him — his children were still young and the middle-aged lawyer possessed no formal musical qualifications. Heaven knows what was going on in his head. I imagine the 'do or die' mantra must have been in there somewhere, perhaps a presentiment or even a first symptom of his long degenerative illness prompting the thought that time was passing. Almost certainly it was the same struggle between yearning and social/familial responsibility that we all experience. But when one is thirty-nine or thereabouts it's tagged a 'mid-life crisis'.

Since this was 1880, and not a hundred years later, Chabrier could not seek the advice of psychiatrists, financial advisors, lifestyle columnists, radio chat shows or self-help books. All would doubtless have told him that his plan was a folly attributable to 'that' time of life. Think of the damage he would have done to his superannuation! In his own time there would have been plenty of anxious muttering from in-laws, friends, the gang at the Home Office.

As it turns out, Chabrier was right to take the punt. His time was short. There would be little more than ten years left for him to follow his passion. And if the doubting Thomases of then — or now — had prevailed, the world would have had one less great composer to tell us something valuable about joy … and life. Chabrier's dilemma, even the decision he took, is common these days; the consequences of that decision decidedly not. They are the glorious musical dividends of a risk-taker. We should all be so lucky to have such a crisis.

The right path to take in life or any endeavour is usually the most obvious: Falling under Wagner's spell was therefore a catalyst that earns our gratitude. Unfortunately, Chabrier's infatuation morphed into attempts to emulate, if not downright imitate, the German master. In spite of his proclivity for wit and the fast-paced stage comedy, for intimacy and the short punchy musical message, he decided to write large dramatic operas with quasi-mythic settings à la *Tristan*: *Gwendoline* (1886), starring the Saxons and the Danes in ninth-century Britain, and *Briséis* (1897), a Christian versus Pagan version of *Sophie's Choice* set even further back in the first century AD and mercifully unfinished. Having jumped in the right car, much time was wasted in driving down the wrong road. Perhaps this was his notion of what a 'serious' composer did. There isn't much modern regard for these long-winded excursions against the grain. What an irony for Chabrier after all his early railing against 'Serious Art'!

To assess a person's worth, look at the quality of their friendships: Chabrier would be at my Ultimate Dinner Party. He may not have had Oscar Wilde's class of wit or Wagner's charisma, but there must have been something about this short, balding, paunchy character that endeared him to many in the artistic milieu of Paris. He fell in with a group of literary types called *Le Parnasse* who maintained a sort of HQ in a café.

An early friend and artistic collaborator was the great poet Paul Verlaine who later wrote a sonnet about him. Painters were conspicuous in his circle and he paid them the supreme compliment of purchasing their works — Monet, Renoir, Cézanne. Manet's famous *A Bar at the Folies-Bergères* used to hang above Chabrier's piano; the painter later died in his arms. He even enjoyed the friendship of other composers like Fauré, Chausson, Saint-Saëns and Massenet; in short, the ones at the time who counted. His close friend Duparc dragged him on that fateful pilgrimage to Munich to hear *Tristan*. Later he was invited by Wagner's widow Cosima to tea in Bayreuth and brought little distinction upon himself by quietly discarding his unwanted cake into a chest of drawers. By all accounts, this glittering assembly weren't treated like mere collectables; these were warm and generous friendships built on mutual esteem. His music is just as endearing and evokes the composer's personality to those who came after.

⌘

In the 1920s, the French composer Francis Poulenc put a coin into an automatic record player in Paris. Out came a piano piece called *Idylle* by Chabrier, whom Poulenc had believed to be a minor composer. He later wrote: '… even today it makes me tremble with emotion to think of the resultant miracle … my music has never forgotten that first kiss … dear Chabrier, how we all love you!'

⌘

On my very first trip to France many years ago I attended a performance of Verdi's opera *The Force of Destiny* (1862) in the old Paris Opéra (the one the Phantom was supposed to have inhabited; the Opéra has since been moved to new high-tech premises over at the Bastille). A full house was enthusiastic about the set designs, based on paintings by Goya, and the conducting of Julius Rudel. At the conclusion of the night, while the tumultuous applause resounded off the glorious Chagall ceiling, I noticed that an elderly patron had left her seat and was walking delicately down the aisle towards the orchestra pit. Arriving at her destination, she gave what I assumed to be an approving pat to the shoulder of the surprised Maestro before turning on her heels and tottering off.

I have been among many warmly applauding audiences over the years but I doubt that I will ever again see a response as heartfelt as that old lady's pat of gratitude.

⸺

We won't linger too much over joy. It is obviously a state that most composers find less interesting than explorations of the darker emotions. In opera the most boring parts occur when characters tell us how happy they are; fortunately, their bliss never lasts long.

Joy's most famous anthem would have to be that of Beethoven's setting of Schiller's *Ode to Joy* in the final movement of his Ninth Symphony (1824). It was a spectacular innovation at the time; the expression of a feeling so great that the traditional instruments-only scoring of a symphony cracked like a redundant Berlin Wall to allow voices to come rushing through. They sang it in Germany to celebrate that very event in 1989 and in Japan there are hundreds of annual performances of the work. Joy is confined in the famous tune to a span of essentially five notes, and yet it seems to open out and enfold the world. (More on Beethoven in **Anger**.)

Another world resounding with joy is evoked in the orchestral suite *The Planets* (1918) by the English-born **Gustav Holst** (1874–1934). Leaving the Earth out and composed before the discovery of Pluto, this serenade to outer space has been frequently used for dramatic signatures in TV shows about war and … well, outer space. *Jupiter, the Bringer of Jollity* is a big galumphing piece whose percolating textures settle down at one point for one of those 'big' tunes that the British love to sing.

Sing of simple joys: The 'all Men become brothers, You millions I embrace you' thing in Beethoven's Ninth might be a bit of a morale booster at football matches but music sets us a more practical example when it sings of life's smaller pleasures. Johann Sebastian Bach composed hundreds of sacred cantatas but my own favourite is a secular one in which a rebellious daughter brags of her fondness — yeah verily, her **addiction** for coffee in the so-called 'Coffee' Cantata (1734). What one hopes to be a more private pleasure is vented by the Swiss-born **Ludwig Senfl** (c1486–1543) in a song about breaking wind in the bath; a relief to the perpetrator but a conversation-stopper at parties I've found.

Drinking is a popular musical topic. Goblets are raised in the tavern scene of many an opera. If the characters are too high-born to nick off to the pub they drink at home with a multitude of friends. In Italian opera a drinking song is a Brindisi; Verdi's *La traviata* features a famous example in Act One. England's **King Henry VIII** (1491–1547) was undoubtedly a popular man, having almost as many friends as he did wives, and he celebrated the good times in a great song called *Pastyme with good companye.*

George Gershwin's (1898–1937) *Promenade* also rejoices under the title *Walking the Dog* and I frequently dedicated broadcasts of the piece to early-morning strollers and their best friends. (Wagner was also nuts about his mutts.) Non-surrogate children feature in operas and instrumental 'nursery' suites; one of the most beautiful being Bizet's *Children's Games* of 1871. The small hero of Rossini's *Song of the Baby* does what babies do so many times a day and reports the 'ca-ca' to Daddy. Perhaps Rossini took some pleasure in infantilism, given that the song features in his late collection *Sins of Old Age*.

We've been feeling pretty good in this narrative so far. Our emotional graph has described an upward spike into the 'excess' zone, granted – but moderation is not a quality that is nurtured during the early phase of a love affair.

Let's do so now by bringing down the curtain on all this effervescence at the mid-point of our programme, turning up the lights and making our way to the bar for some conviviality and light refreshments. The lessons in love are not all we need to know for safe conduct through life. It is time to take some time out from all this passion to distil some practical advice on things outside love – again, from our friends' cocked-up examples. Enjoy your drink. In the drama of romance, as in concerts, things usually become darker in the second half.

⊷ SOME MUSICAL LIFE TIPS ⊶

"… the purpose of writing music? … simply a
way to wake up to the very life we're living …"
JOHN CAGE, 1957

NO SPEED LIMITS: It's tempting to imagine composers tinkering endlessly over their operas and symphonies. All that detail must take some fine-tuning. And all those notes! Leonardo da Vinci applied those never-quite-finishing touches to his diminutive portrait of the Mona Lisa for years. Surely an immense construct like Handel's *Messiah* must have demanded a similar feat of endurance?

Well, no. Apparently it is easier to praise Jesus in sound than to paint a smile. In 1741, Handel composed *Messiah* end to end between 22 August and 14 September; just under three-and-a-half weeks. He slowed to a canter with his next oratorio, *Samson*, which emerged from labour six weeks later on 29 October. Both occupy a very full evening in the hearing. I remember playing a four-minute chorus from his oratorio *Israel in Egypt* — the whole of which took just under the month of October 1738 to find its way to paper — remarking that this elaborate piece probably took up most of a day's work, right down to the viola's last semiquaver. One of Handel's librettists, the Reverend Thomas Morell, might well have claimed a miracle had taken place when he delivered the text for an aria, ducked out of the room for a twinkle and returned three minutes later to find that Handel had already completed the vocal line.

Mozart was not only just as fast but could apparently do other things at the same time. In a variation of the ventriloquist who drinks water while his dummy talks, he wrote the Overture to his opera *Don Giovanni* while quaffing punch and chatting with his wife the night before the opera's premiere in 1787. Next time you're in a music shop take a squiz at the Overture in full score. It would take an ordinary human being more than a night just to copy it out. Mozart's hand is faster than our eye.

But when it came to just getting around the track the Italian composers of *bel canto* opera in the early 1800s took the bends better than anybody. Theirs was truly opera *espresso*. The opera world of those days was fast and loose with new pieces churning through provincial houses at an incredible rate. Composers would receive commissions a handful of weeks before opening night. And if the work was a flop? Well, an Italianate shrug of the shoulders and on to the next new piece, due for performance in a month. Rossini's *The Barber of Seville* occupied him for just thirteen days in 1816 — although sections of it (including its Overture) were merely recycled from earlier failures. No sense in letting an audience's disapproval kill good material after all. The *Barber* was also a famous first night disaster (see **Triumph**) but survived its close shave. Rossini's compatriot **Gaetano Donizetti** (1797–1848) is said to have knocked off his comedy classic *The Elixir of Love* (1832) in eight days.

Other composers were happier to substitute one big egg (like an opera) with many smaller ones — songs, for instance. **Franz Schubert** (1797–1828), **Robert Schumann** (1810–1856) and **Hugo Wolf** (1860–1903), three of the greatest composers of German song (or *lieder*) were like pigs in mud if they could set several texts a *day*. I now feel decidedly uncomfortable about the speed at which I'm writing this book. Do me a favour and read quickly.

Never neglect home security: This is even more applicable when the immediate family is keen to hasten your demise. The great French violinist and composer **Jean-Marie Leclair** (1697–1764) fell upon hard domestic times late in life when he parted from his wife and set up in his own small house in one of Paris' less salubrious suburbs. One night he was stabbed to death on his own doorstep. In a scenario Agatha Christie would have loved, the *gendarmerie* settled on three suspects — the gardener, Leclair's wife and his rival violinist nephew. Most evidence pointed to the latter but the case was never brought to trial.

It's a young person's world: As we all know, life may be faster now but it was shorter then. Even though demographic research tells us that people tend to come to

classical music later in life it would be a mistake to extrap-
olate the assumption that its writing was the activity of sen-
iors. It is a hoot to watch Mick Jagger strut on stage, or
Michael Jackson harness cosmetic technology in his
journey towards Peter Pan. There's nothing wrong with getting on a bit — in fact, I've recently taken to it myself —
but it's amusing to note that some of today's time-tested
messengers of musical youth culture are now older than
many of my own pin-ups ever were.

The life-spans of composers, while not always unusual for
the times in which they lived, make exasperating reading
today. Mozart — thirty-five; Chopin, Mendelssohn,
Gershwin — all under forty; Schubert — thirty-one. The
obviously frail Italian Giovanni Pergolesi, one of the most
successful composers of the eighteenth century — twenty-
six. And one of the most exciting new talents of the nineteenth century, the Spaniard Arriaga, made it to nineteen, for
heaven's sake. Those who did kick on did so with a notoriety acquired early. The Russian **Igor Stravinsky**
(1882–1971) wrote his punkish picture of a young girl
dancing herself to death (and one of the watershed works of
the twentieth century), *The Rite of Spring* (1913), at the age
of thirty. Berlioz' swirling musical vortex of lovelorn hallucinations, the *Fantastic Symphony*, bled onto the page when
he was twenty-six. Hardly a crow's foot among them — yet
we still feel that maturity is the passport to their world.

...But it's never too late to start: Tchaikovsky (see
Sadness) was twenty-one when he began a serious music
education; the Frenchman **Ernest Chausson** (1855–1899)

shopped around in writing and drawing, even taking a law degree, before starting formal tuition in music at the age of twenty-four. Erik Satie (see **Excess & Obsession**) decided that piano-playing in smoky Parisian cafés wasn't enough training and went back to music school at the age of thirty-nine. Remember — *your* speed is always the right speed.

Avoid public transport: Music history would suggest that the past can catch up with one in quite unexpected ways. Composer **Isaac Nathan** (1790–1864) enjoyed a good run of removing himself from sticky situations — usually financial ones. Creditors drove him from his native England into Wales in his late twenties. It is possible he was a secret agent for George IV, masquerading as the King's music librarian; a sort of early nineteenth-century James Bond with crotchets. Consorting with the aristocracy must have earned him a few confidences given that his most conspicuous London operatic stage success was the 1823 *Sweethearts and Wives*. Eventually he was ruined through 'unspecified services' for William IV and emigrated to Australia in 1841, where he became the uncrowned king of the Sydney colonial musical scene; composing, teaching, annotating Aboriginal music, and writing about everything from the arts to boxing. His days of courtly espionage behind him, Nathan penned the alarmingly titled *Merry Freaks in Troublous Times* (1843); one assumes that casting difficulties prevented a complete production. I feel sure we could surmount those problems these days.

Isaac Nathan didn't watch his step and met his accidental

end under the wheels of a horse-drawn tram in 1864.

...But drive carefully! Puccini and Ravel managed to have nasty accidents even in cars proceeding at a slow speed. The unfortunate Chausson mentioned above, having started late, proceeded to finish early when he fell off his pushbike aged forty-four.

Remember — these are always the bad old days: Two sisters are engaged to officers who make a wager with a cynical old bachelor about their fiancées' fidelity. Interestingly, it is the bachelor who maintains that women are incapable of fidelity — as he says (in Italian), 'Così fan tutte' ... all women behave like this.

So how quickly can morals be subverted and the obligations of fidelity be swamped by a surfeit of suggestions in foreign accents and a set of tanned loins? And if our bleary-eyed guinea pigs do stray, what does that say about the shallowness and sexual opportunism of today's society?

A set-up is staged wherein the officers are suddenly called off to war only to be supplanted by the equally abrupt appearance of two swarthy Albanians who are, of course, the same officers in turbans and a little boot polish on their faces. They begin to chat up each other's girlfriend and this partner-swapping exercise pays off within the day when wedding plans are announced after heavy petting.

This isn't an Italian version of one of those 'reality' television shows in which happy couples are taken to a modern Garden of Eden and separated, only to be tempted by a procession of beautiful strangers under the watchful eye of the camera. It is the plot of Mozart's opera of 1790,

Così fan tutte, with the libretto again by Lorenzo da Ponte. So much for old-time constancy. We should never believe the cant about a 'purer' age put about by parents and other self-appointed moralists. Mozart reminds us that human impulse and our incapacity to control it all the time hasn't changed for hundreds of years. The remedy? A good laugh, a sincere effort at repentance, and an acceptance of our predictable fallibility.

You don't need a degree: As someone who never completed high school or attended university I have great sympathy for the autodidact. Let's face it, today's big hard world is awash with multi-degreed graduates and a person without their validating piece of paper is about as useful as mere Air on a G-string. The same holds true for aspiring 'serious' composers. Their armoury of technical knowledge has to be so comprehensive that it can be front-end loaded only in university lecture rooms. Young composers come complete with their 'papers', rather like hopeful emigrés at a border crossing, or a pedigree spaniel.

To this our musical faces of the past say — have faith in your own powers and the refining crucible of life. I can suggest no motivational techniques save that of comparison, for most great composers never emerged from a classroom with that degree in hand. Some were almost entirely self-taught. Don't fall about too much at this proof of their genius. Dabbing notes on a page of staves is nothing more than learning a system and the basic blocks of Western music notation aren't that complex.

Our old friend Georg Philipp Telemann (see **Excess &**

Obsession) was more celebrated and successful than Bach during his lifetime. A pastor's son, he is said as a boy to have learned to play the flute, violin and zither before he could read a note. He soon taught himself notation and acquired style by studying the scores of others. I should say style(s), because Telemann became so technically proficient that he could switch around and write in the German, French or Italian fashions of the day. He must have picked up music as a child picks up language.

Richard Wagner is perhaps the most breathtaking example of a composer who made his own way. A late starter in music and thereafter a poor performer at school once the mania had bitten him, Wagner scraped a couple of years of lessons from a Leipzig local when in his late teens. The rest of the time was spent alone making his own way through music textbooks, or (more importantly) writing out the music of his musical hero Beethoven.

Jacques Offenbach (1819–1880) put the crotchets into the can-can — yes, that's his tune — and supplied the heady musical champagne for mid-nineteenth-century France with operettas such as *Orpheus in the Underworld* (1858). You could credit him as the pioneer of what became the twentieth-century musical. And yet this classic Gallic entertainer was born in Germany, the son of a cantor, only going to Paris in search of formal tuition when he was fourteen. His studies at the Paris Conservatoire lasted just a year. Knocking around in the pit orchestras of local theatres proved a far greater schooling for the teenage cellist. **Edward Elgar** (1857–1934) found himself as a composer only in his forties (see **Sadness**). He taught himself the violin and composition within the conducive surroundings of the family music-shop but received his best practical experience while conducting the band in a local lunatic asylum. Slow and steady wins, they say; when he finally hit his mother lode it yielded symphonies, concertos and a wealth of incidental music that is still underestimated outside his native England.

Learning on the job was the reality for the Brazilian **Heitor Villa-Lobos** (1887–1959), who picked up some tips about the cello from his civil servant father before the latter's death when Heitor was only ten. From then on he was a working musician, busking in the streets of Rio, playing with theatre companies and doing the rounds of cafés. He made some trips into the jungles of the Brazilian interior to suss out the indigenous music and eventually enrolled at Rio's National Music Institute. By then it was too late; he lasted in the lecture-rooms for only a year and was then back on his lonesome road. He does a great impression of a steam train in *The Little Train of the Caipira* (1930), a shunting/whistling/wheezing vignette from his series called the *Bachianas brasileiras*: in a nutshell, Bach meets Brazil.

Honourable mentions go to **Chabrier**, our star in **Joy**, who dabbled in music while working as a French civil servant, and a self-taught Dane of whom I'm very fond, **Peter Erasmus Lange-Müller** (1850–1926), who was spared the drudgery of a professional working life by inherited wealth and could tinker away at his music on a country estate.

Just do it: Many years ago I was obsessed with the ambition of conducting orchestras and decamped to London just after my nineteenth birthday to observe my heroes at work. Prevailing upon the English Maestro Raymond Leppard to let me watch a rehearsal, I asked him afterwards for advice on making a career with the baton.

'If you want to conduct,' he said, 'then … conduct.'

In the silence that followed I realised that he was not going to recommend a course of study, a great conservatorium or even a stick-wielding guru. Just go and do it? I thought this a great recipe for charlatanism; sure enough there were moments in later years, as I sat in recording control booths watching people self-immolate on the podium, when I wondered if too many had been keen to take Leppard's advice. There was also the matter of logistics. Merely waving one's arms about is all very well but generally ineffectual without several musicians sitting nearby who are prepared to follow your direction. This is where the environment of a music school comes in handy these days; they tend to be populated by instrumentalists.

Leppard's advice was good, though. The process of 'doing' such an exposed activity implies the presence of a range of skills besides plain musicality, and nobler qualities than a liking for telling others what to do (as opposed to real leadership). Sure, there are snake-oil salespeople in the profession, but there are other maestros who seem to have materialised with their astonishing ability out of thin-air, stepping down from the organ loft (like Leopold

Stokowski) or up from the orchestra's cello section (like Arturo Toscanini).

This was back in the ages before self-help manuals or motivational weekends. Were they running on five-year plans or constant visualisation? In a sense, yes. Conductors sign multi-year contracts so their working future is always structured for the medium-term, and they need to have an ideal performance of a symphony resonating in their heads before giving the first downbeat. In the end, good old passion is their fuel — and it certainly agrees with them. While music history is brimful of short-lived composers, it's also chockers with maestro Methuselahs. Maybe conductors really do feed on the vital energies that soon-depleted composers give, or maybe it's all that aerobic arm-waving.

Always choose built-ins: Charles Alkan (1813–1888) was a recluse. The French pianist and composer was so crippled by shyness that he gave only six recitals in the space of thirty-five years. He vanished from public view in between and kept to himself, leaving no record of large parts of his life. Alkan dressed like a cleric and matched his demeanour with the assembly of a large theological library kept in free-standing bookcases, one assumes: he is said to have been killed when one of them fell on him.

It's OK to worry about pimples: He was described by Aldous Huxley as 'the voluptuous dentist' but it seems that the Russian pianist/composer **Alexander Scriabin** (1872–1915) could have been more diligent in the oral hygiene department. He was probably born eighty years too early; his ideas about attaining ecstasy through 'global consciousness' and 'cosmic regeneration' would have won him a few adherents in a 1970s California compound, while his attempts at a complete synthesis of music, colour and image might have been achieved with the advent of CD-ROM. He sported an exquisitely-turned moustache but there was trouble brewing under that facial hair. An unattended pimple grew into full-blown septicaemia which killed him at the age of forty-three.

Oranges are dangerous: A personal reminiscence; years ago I played an urchin in a production of the Czech operatic comedy *The Bartered Bride*, by **Bedrich Smetana** (1824–1884) (another syphilitic, poor man). At this barely pubescent stage in my life I was much in demand as a 'stage-filler', playing jockeys, dancing shepherds, urchins, very small policemen and crippled boys. Our stage for this particular show had limited wing space and the chorus of happy Bohemian peasants had been given no dressing room. They resorted to making their costume changes on stage behind the 'flat', or propped-up facade of the village inn. The sound of mysterious rustling issuing from the inn was masked by the vigorous playing of the large student orchestra in the pit.

The liveliest part of the show was the 'Dance of the Comedians', a rollicking folk-ballet complete with spinning couples, a walking bear and a juggler of oranges. To make way for this entourage, the chorus graciously retired to the inn. The juggler led on the dancers and suffered one of those unfortunate nervous slips of the hand, showering the stage in a citrus cascade. One by one the oranges rolled forward into the pit, bombing the surprised players and breaking a viola. The orchestra whirred on and the stage was now full of urchins and dancing peasants. I watched in morbid fascination as the cloud of feet moved inexorably towards the single remaining orange glowing like a traffic light. And it happened, of course. A slip, a sudden lurch backward into the delicately poised inn, and with an almighty crash the audience was treated to nineteenth-century village maidens clutching their 1970s brassieres.

The curtain was brought down on the now flattened village square and the inn hastily resurrected. I've heard a number of stories about the audience pelting the stage with fruit; this is the only instance I know of an attempt in the opposite direction.

Watch the mushrooms: Johann Schobert (c1735–1767), not to be confused with Franz Schubert, was admired and imitated by the young Mozart. Thank heavens Wolfgang didn't follow in the older man's culinary footsteps. A promising career was cut short when the composer picked and cooked some wild mushrooms against the advice of a local Parisian tavern-keeper. The poisoned lunch carried away Schobert along with his wife and child. *Always listen to the locals.*

Deciding when to fold 'em: It would seem that good ideas — as much as good times — can come to an end. Often these shutdowns are merely a phase; patience and acceptance are required to quietly endure their passage. Because the act of creation is meant to be driven exclusively by the whim and generosity of the Muse, and because it makes for a good story, we believe that composers just have to write music because they simply can't help themselves. Death is supposedly the reason for the end of a composer's career.

In fact many composers have had periods of fallowness; for some, inactivity merged into retirement. The American **Charles Ives** (1874–1954) wrote music only when he wasn't making a fortune running his own insurance company. One day in 1926, tinkering upstairs in his house with crotchets much as other men would be out with the spare parts in the shed, he came downstairs with tears in his eyes and said that he couldn't compose any more. The lights had gone out just like that. His discovery as a pioneering figure in music happened after; in 1947 his music won the Pulitzer Prize. But not a single new note could be coaxed out of him. (One day try out his 1908 piece for small orchestra called *The Unanswered Question*.) Ives got on with his life and didn't spend his time mourning the shutdown of that creative spark. When it is over …

Have you often felt that the times have passed you by, that somehow, just by staying true to yourself, you have dropped out of the loop? The Finn **Jean Sibelius** (1865–1957) was considered one of the major musical figures of the world by the end of the First World War. His symphonies eerily evoke the chill, sparse landscapes of his homeland. But by the 1920s the signposts of his old musical world were being torn out. Nobody was writing the sort of music he liked anymore. Not that he had stayed the same either; his last big orchestral work, *Tapiola* (1926) (which you'll need to listen to in an overcoat, such is the blast of icy wind from the music) feels like the stylistic last stop on the Sibelius line. Perhaps he felt — what else can I do? And the answer (a brave one) was — nothing. He put down his pen and lived for thirty more years, increasingly venerated around the world.

Never be too emphatic: The Italian-born **Jean-Baptiste Lully** (1632–1687) ruled the musical roost at the palace of Versailles and was a favourite of Louis XIV; he was therefore very used to having his own way. One day he was conducting a new Te Deum setting to celebrate the King's recovery from a recent illness. Forget the nifty little waved baton; Lully's method of conducting was to literally beat time by pounding a wooden staff on the floor. In a moment of excessive enthusiasm he rammed the stick through his foot. The injury became gangrenous and killed him. Moral — *the mightiest can be impaled on their authority*.

If you've heard it all before there is a good reason: A tale of music and the emotions. You can refer to my motorised pilgrimage through northern Spain in the **Freedom & Release** chapter. These were splendid days of silence, for I resisted the temptation to be kept company by Spanish talkback radio, feeling that all the incomprehensible gabbling would clutter the surprising emptiness of that part of the country. I had come here for the pictures, not the words. Taking a holiday from Beethoven and the rest of the troupe seemed a good idea too, if I was to fulfil one of the requirements of pilgrimage and discard the habits of another life. Several times I reached for the tuning dial on the radio to begin a search for whatever northern Spain had to offer as a classical music station before returning trembling fingers to the steering wheel. Little did I realise that I was inducing some form of musical malnutrition.

It was a warm May afternoon and lunch was in order. I stopped in a small town near Burgos which seemed unnaturally quiet; siesta was under way. One establishment was open and it looked strangely salubrious in this rustic setting with the odd chicken pecking about in sight of its elegant windows. Inside its old stone walls were large cloth-topped tables and cutlery set with military precision; those starched serviettes that one needs to prise apart with a jemmy providing testimony of a serious attitude. The room was devoid of people, except for a young girl loitering at the reception desk. At that moment I decided there was no more tragic sight in the world than a solitary diner in a large restaurant. But since this was Spain, I reasoned, no pictures of this little scene with my incriminating solitude would find their way back to Australia.

When the *senorita* came over I ordered the wrong meal in a language unknown to both of us. Settling back, I noticed that the sound system was operating at a discreet whisper — a wonderful development in itself and well worth emulating by any restaurant if they must insist on having any music at all — and that the music was, God bless it, Vivaldi's *Four Seasons*.

This ambush disarmed me; my faculty for disregarding music too familiar was suspended. I reheard the music with rapt attention, allowing the seasons to rain and shine over my table. This really is very good, I thought. The clarity of texture, the assurance of the writing, the vividness of the swooping strings, the pictures of barking dogs, hunting horns, savage winds, spotting rains and slippery ice made me, well, putty in Vivaldi's imagination. Its beauty was shameless and generous. I was suddenly overwhelmed by the fact that the old asthmatic Red Priest of Venice could make me feel so good — so *thankful* — more than two hundred and fifty years after his death.

Get a handle on yourself, cautioned the Anglo-Saxon inside me, you're starting to lose it. This was true; I was actually weeping in a deserted Spanish restaurant because of the music playing on the sound system. The chrome-strengthened serviette couldn't help me now. I dabbed at my face with one sleeve under cover of the single sheet menu which curled back to reveal my travail to the wait-ress as she approached with a bread roll. No questions were asked, but she showed concern for the just-baked crust by depositing it at a distance from the moistening grasp of my fingers.

I have no recollection of the food but I will never forget the epiphanic occasion. It was an unexpected reminder of music's power to trigger emotion and what a completely intuitive process listening should be. It also reminded me of how much I love the stuff; even the stuff that is hackneyed for some people. Familiarity seems to promote a sense of disengagement akin to what a politician must feel after the fiftieth handshake at a fundraiser. But great music keeps coming around for reasons other than the whim of fashion and it sometimes takes an unexpected hearing to reveal its quality.

Composers on form just make every stroke a winner. I'm all in favour of so-called orchestral 'pops' concerts with (for example) Rossini's *William Tell* Overture, Grieg's Piano Concerto, Beethoven's Fifth and Tchaikovsky's *1812*. The music is still fabulous and audiences look well-fed as they leave. This is music's Sunday roast: comfort food that is always good for you. You can be adventurous again on Monday.

Always carry a Swiss Army knife: Apropos of music in restaurants, I was touring country New South Wales with a visiting English pianist many years ago, recording some of his recitals along the way for radio broadcasts. Our lunchtime restaurant visit in one town was marred by the imposition of some ghastly muzak which was no doubt intended to incite enthusiasm for the food. Our polite request to turn it off (we were the only customers) was interpreted as a slur on the good taste of management and the intruding noise was instead turned *up*. The pianist mentioned that he was prepared for such occasions and excused himself to go to the lavatory. During his brief absence the aural scabies disappeared as if by magic, causing puzzlement among the floor staff who began tapping on the side panel of a troublesome amplifier. The real cause was more sinister; the returning pianist flashed me a glimpse of his Swiss Army knife and with a nod of his head indicated the imperceptibly severed speaker cables snaking up the wall.

When it is OK to talk to strangers: This same pianist was allegedly psycho-kinetic. He claimed to perform certain pieces under the guidance of the composer; Beethoven would be right there with, or *inside* him, guiding those fingers. I took this claim with a degree of cynicism until deciding to make an interval visit to his dressing room one night to offer the customary words of encouragement. There was no response to my knocking on his unlocked door. When I eased it open rather gingerly, I realised he was in earnest conversation with … no-one. He was holding open the music of Liszt's *Transcendental Studies* (1851) on his lap and pointing at certain bars while gazing into mid-air, asking, '… and here? What would you like me to do here?', then pausing for the inaudible reply. This was a consultation too important to interrupt. I crept away. He played with great … authority that night.

Not long after this a charming listener from Adelaide tracked me down to make an urgent confession, telling me that she had received approval to do so from certain 'advisors'. She was a perfectly lucid middle-aged woman with two adolescent sons and a husband who put in too many hours at a refrigeration company. She had known nothing about music and had been understandably disconcerted when, writing a letter to her father several years before, her pen had traced out the phrase 'I am Ludwig van Beethoven'. After making investigations about the identity of her invisible pen-pal she resigned herself to his increasingly frequent visits; in fact, she felt a strong attraction to him. Their discussions through the medium of the pen became more intimate. Beethoven was upsetting her marriage. He introduced her to some of his other-wordly colleagues and she began making new friendships. Schubert was a wonderful shopping companion, she said. There was an embarrassing luncheon at which some of her girlfriends began talking disparagingly about homosexuality, little realising that Tchaikovsky was sitting at their table.

But Beethoven was closest to her and eventually he made suggestions as to which recordings of his works she should buy. As she said, he seemed such a lovely person that she wanted to acquaint herself with his music. The Seventh Symphony (1812) was a favourite of hers. The composer recommended Karajan over Bernstein. Who was she to quibble? Their dialogue up to this point had been expressed solely via the pen. Once, and only once, did she experience a visual manifestation. The sight of his 'lovely' face was the clincher. She decided to run away with him. Nevertheless she was uncertain about how news of this unorthodox relationship would be received by her friends. I had been sought out for counsel; what should she do?

I responded that one had to look at past form, and on that basis the signs for the future weren't encouraging (see **Anger**). Sure, Beethoven had probably resolved some personal problems in his new plane of existence. The deafness was certainly no longer an issue. But the composer had a history of being attracted to married women while being very judgemental about other people's morality; moreover, his real mistress would always be his work. It would be no fun being elbowed aside to make room for a sonata. Far safer, I said, to put this down to experience and opt for friendship. He may not have her body, but there would always be the handwriting.

The advice was accepted and acted upon; when we next spoke, she and Ludwig had worked it out. And when I flew out of Adelaide, she met me at the airport and pressed into my hands a small sheaf of envelopes containing letters from her 'circle' — Beethoven included. I was instructed to open them only when I was airborne, and to never divulge their contents to anyone.

And I never have.

⤙ ANGER ⤚

We come now to the most dangerous part of the book, for if the fragile vessel of a romance sustains some hairline cracks from the distorting emotions of earlier chapters, anger is the one that will burst it apart. At the time the person losing it will think of their anger as a corrective in one of those weird bursts of self-justification. This applies on just about any scale, which is why countries can so confidently start a war. But the sad truth is that little 'snap' is a destroyer.

I'VE NEVER MET anyone who hasn't confessed to losing their temper or simply getting a bit shirty now and then. (Mind you, I haven't met the Dalai Lama either.) It just seems to be a part of our overall package. Perhaps it even contributes to the 'flavour' of our personalities, like the infusion from the dregs in a bottle of wine. No dregs make a dreary drop.

So if there is anything at all that makes me tetchy, it is the suggestion by any would-be psychologist that I'm carrying repressed anger. The 'analysis' is so obvious in its banality that it makes me want to kick them. Of course, I don't. Instead I might take refuge later in Beethoven's *Egmont* Overture (1810) and let the orchestra give the music a good thumping — as invited by the score. Sometimes — but not often — I can understand why certain testosterone-riddled drivers turn their vehicles into boom-boxes.

For this is the great surprise about classical music; it is not a sedative. It does not engage us by dulling our reactions. It *does* perform the useful meditative function of opening the windows on certain parts of ourselves and allowing us to observe them one at a time. But frequently the view is not so good. Why should it be? As you are discovering, composers (like us) were not entirely serene. One could make the pat suggestion that they all carried around some repressed anger. It had to come out somewhere and a sheet of empty manuscript paper must have been a tantalising target. You can't be arrested for assaulting your own symphony. Things do get a little hotter, though, when we suspect the music is assaulting *us* (see below).

So while listening to and engaging with good music can be a useful catharsis, that doesn't necessarily lead us to the conclusion that it makes us into better people. Don't ever accept the implication from a musical snob that they are a more highly developed being because they 'understand' Bach — or Stockhausen — and you don't. Conversely, maintain your composure when an idiot condemns the Stockhausen — or Bach — they haven't yet understood. At the very least, try not to kick them.

The demolition of the notion of classical music as 'ennobling' was effected forcibly by Stanley Kubrick's 1971 film *A Clockwork Orange*, based on the novel by Anthony Burgess. (I'm a Kubrick fan, it must be said, and he'll be back later.) The portrayal of 'ultra-violence' gave it a notoriety that continues to this day. Even more confronting was the use of Beethoven's music ('lovely Ludwig van') as an aural incitement for the principal gang-leader's violent fantasies and rampages. This raised the prospect that, somehow, good music could also be bad for you.

In the end, music's effect is up to the listener. I feel confident in predicting you won't be turned into a psychopath by Beethoven's Ninth Symphony. At a concert of the work I attended recently there were no signs of scuffles at the drinks bar during intermission. But Beethoven remains one of the supreme figures in Western music nearly two hundred years after his death because the power of his music reaches deep down into the dregs of our bottle.

> *"I will seize Fate by the throat …"*
> LUDWIG VAN BEETHOVEN, 1801

… and in the red corner, there he is — shortish (165 cm), pugnacious, carrying quite a gut at the weigh-in and doing a great job of filling his ringside spittoon. His opponent in the dark corner, the trim but diaphanous spectre of Fate, is looking less confident after having delivered some nasty but effective blows to the composer's ears in the early rounds. The Blaster from Bonn has bounced back from the ropes with the gloves off and has had the unbeaten champion on the mat for the greater part of this fight.

Like all great fighters, Beethoven is driven by anger. You can see it in contemporary portraits, particularly as he gets older; that 'I'm as mad as Hell …' look in the eyes, the rebellious hair. You can feel it in his music, emphatic as a fist slamming the table. It's the anger we all feel at some point in our lives over our unfair treatment at the hands of Fate.

I'm not talking about petty irritations here — although Beethoven could blow a gasket over those too, as in his piano piece *Rage over a Lost Penny* (1795). No; this is the big one. Everyone cheers for Ludwig in this supreme contest because he's up there slugging it out for all of us.

Some philosophies and religions espouse a more passive response to some of life's low blows. We're supposed to just take the punches and let the bad moment pass. This was not Beethoven's way. He would never go gently into anyone's good night.

You know how the bout ends, of course. Fate wins the struggle through sheer endurance. But Beethoven would keep an uppercut in reserve right through to the end in

1827; it is said that on his deathbed he shook his fist in defiance at a thunderclap as a storm raged outside.

***

Ludwig van Beethoven is an essential but nevertheless difficult life guide in a book such as this. Being 'guided' at all presupposes an element of adaptation, a degree of bending with the wind. Ludwig fully expected the world to bend to *him*. This made for a great musical outcome but a few rude shocks in life's other departments. The very impossibility of appearing to be flippant about Beethoven is a measure of our respect for his achievement, but it also shows the extent to which he has been mythologised by succeeding generations of composers and audiences.

The popular notion of the 'artist', or (to be more pejorative) one of those 'creative types' is still modelled after Beethoven's example. Indeed, he was one of the first to describe himself as an 'artist'. You know the image: the wild-haired dysfunctional rebel, cocking a snook at the 'old ways' of thinking and behaviour, a wild cannon at social gatherings, unkempt (a reflection of external disorder versus pure inner vision) and unhygienic, creating world-shattering fancies in an isolated garret.

The image has been building up since before Beethoven's death, but we still cherish it as an effective role-model for several generations of rock musicians, all frowning and venting their spleen on MTV. (To be an 'angry young man'

— or woman — in contemporary arts is to be perceived as violently creative and iconoclastic.)

This fashionable discontent — what we call the 'artistic temperament' — is a far cry from Beethoven. His was the authentic angst. But let's get things in proportion. Ludwig is of paramount importance not because he convinces us that he alone is suffering on a cosmic scale; instead, he reassures us that we're *all* in the basket. What's more, he says, life may be lousy for us, but the situation can be turned around by some healthy lunges at Fate's throat.

Beethoven is classical music's motivational speaker, and the message is uniquely empowering. Orchestras know this. Beethoven festivals with all the symphonies and concertos are still sure-fire crowd pullers; for many, he is classical music's genuine article. As I write, the Australian Chamber Orchestra, hot on the heels of press reports detailing management instability and a nasty annual deficit, are opening their new season with Beethoven's *Eroica* Symphony (1805) — no doubt a coincidence, but a good dramatic one. Take THAT, ye doubters!

Watch the audience at the end of a Beethoven concert. You might even catch a bit of sympathetic fist-waving from the executives in the crowd who know that they're going to nail that deal in the morning after the pep-talk of Beethoven's Fifth Symphony (1808). Tired concert goers suddenly develop straight backs. They bolt for the trains before the applause ends with a renewed sense of purpose. Not to do so would somehow be letting Beethoven down, because he has generously shown us the power of the individual will in an unsympathetic world.

While Father Bach advises us to lay low because it will all come right when you die, Ludwig yells that the time for action is now. He's hunting big game but the trophies aren't material ones — well, apart from a decent plate of veal now and then. The preservation of integrity, the natural rule of freedom; all good democratic goals. And no guns, please; just a good steady forward march — but don't spare the headbutts.

Do we end up being happy? Perhaps that's not the point, even though Beethoven's Ninth (and last) Symphony ends with the world singing an Ode to Joy. Mere happiness is not a feeling that pervades Beethoven's finales, although the end of his Sixth Symphony (1808), known as the 'Pastoral', comes close. Rather, the process — the *living* — is the thing. You've probably read something like this before in various books of Eastern philosophy. It's far more inspiring to actually hear it enacted in sound.

The English conductor **Sir Thomas Beecham** (1879–1961) apparently blamed Beethoven for all the 'wrath' later to come in music. The inference from such a remark is that music was quite 'nice' until this unkempt German came along. Much as I admire Beecham, it's what one would expect from someone who probably overdid the *eau de toilette*. Beethoven's music has an almost unprecedented physicality about it, exuding its own sweat; naturally we get a whiff now and then. But these meta-physical workouts were often propelled by anger and, as you'll see, he had a lot to work through …

1. Your childhood was a mess: Ludwig was baptised on 17 December 1770 in Bonn, Germany. His father, a lack-lustre tenor at the local court, was a drunkard who both pro-moted and resented his eldest surviving son's talent. The household was very possibly a violent one. Beethoven also felt that his mother wasn't too affectionate with him. Sickness may have been the cause; tuberculosis killed her when he was sixteen. The family fortunes went into rapid decline as his father's drinking increased, jeopardising his employment.

In such a vortex, the eighteen-year-old took charge in 1789, petitioning for half his father's court salary in order to support two younger brothers so that Dad wouldn't oth-erwise go through it at the local tavern. When Beethoven senior died just three years later, Ludwig didn't so much as mention the fact in his diary.

Now, anyone would emerge from such disastrous brushes with parental authority with what they call 'baggage'. Beethoven had a truckload. For instance, he had real problems with authority figures, be they well-meaning teachers (like **Franz Joseph Haydn** (1732–1809), with whom Beethoven studied for a year and then disparaged later in life), or princes (see 3 below). These were hardly career-boosting qualities to have at a time when patronage by the aristocracy was still a composer's best chance at a regular meal ticket. Beethoven would have been a Pandora's Box on any modern psychiatrist's couch, assuming he could have heard the questions, which brings us to …

2. You're about to crack it big as a musician and then your hearing goes: This is where Fate almost delivers an early knockout. There is Beethoven in 1790s Vienna (having moved to the big smoke), beginning to carve out a real name for himself as a pianist capable of astonishing improvisations — if something of a string-breaker. At this stage, he was truly Society's darling; or at least, its favourite party pianist, playing in the salons of wealthy homes, and later making some successful appearances at events new to Vienna — public concerts. His list of students included young Hungarian countesses, he enjoyed the hospitality of the nobility during the summer at their country estates, publishers were vying for his work (his first couple of piano concertos and early chamber music date from this period). The money was coming in quite nicely. In his late twenties, he was the Bonn boy made bonny.

But even during these early salad days Beethoven must have noticed something awry with his hearing. By 1801 his deafness had already become severe enough to make normal social discourse difficult; conversation at parties was next to impossible. The most savage irony was that this decline in function of the tools of his trade coincided with Beethoven's own awareness of the rapid development of his powers. His depression was overwhelming. In 1802, while on a futile recuperative break in a village outside Vienna, he penned a long letter to his two brothers now known as the 'Heiligenstadt Testament'. Part will, part farewell to life (although rejecting the notion of suicide), it details his personal devastation over his illness: '… as the autumn leaves fall and wither, likewise hope has faded for me.' He was thirty-one.

The constant droning of tinnitus was a torture for Beethoven over the next dozen years. By 1815 he was practically stone deaf and soon after friends would have to 'talk' to him by writing in conversation books. When the Ninth Symphony premiered in 1824 the composer was completely unaware of the audience's enthusiastic reception and had to be turned around to acknowledge the applause. I must say I find this one of music history's most poignant moments.

3. People less deserving than you end up with the lot: We have all felt like victims in life's conspiracy and Beethoven was no exception. But at a time when composers (and indeed most creative artists) were still having to depend on aristocratic largesse, Beethoven was one of the first to declare that mere class was subordinate to talent. He was one of the first standard-bearers of the Romantic ideal of the Artist as Hero. Even as the Austrian Prince Karl Lichnowsky offered Beethoven money, encouragement and performance opportunities, the composer could haughtily remind his benefactor in an 1806 letter that 'there are and will be thousands of princes. There is only one Beethoven.'

This is inspiring self-belief but not helpful if one wants to be, say, an Arab diplomat.

4. You have no success with women: Undoubtedly related to point 2 above and the extent to which it continued to shape Beethoven's behaviour. Being a hearing-impaired member of the lower classes didn't qualify one as Vienna's Bachelor of the Year where whole pedigrees were at stake; added to which Beethoven's personality made it impossible for even male friends to live with him. There is no doubt he desperately wanted a life partner; his one opera — and magnificent it is, too — *Fidelio* (1805) literally sings the praises of married love. But the women he wanted didn't want him, or were not in a position where they could have him. One, at least, was already married — the likely recipient of Beethoven's famous 1812 letter to 'the Immortal Beloved' found among his papers after his death. This represents a sad pivotal moment in the composer's life, as it would in anyone's life; the moment when one realises, or decides, that there is no further likelihood of fully reciprocated love. Small wonder that Beethoven plunged into depression and wrote virtually nothing for years before deciding (as he had in dealing with his deafness) that once again, Art must fill the void. He wrote in his journal in 1816: '… you may be a man no longer … for you there is no longer happiness except in yourself, in your art.'

5. Someone you admire lets you down: Beethoven was a great fan of Napoleon and a supporter of the Little General's campaign for a French Republic. When he began work on his Third Symphony in 1803 it bore the title

'Bonaparte'. This is an epic work: the longest symphony written at that time and one that detonates so many musical conventions; I often think of the brushwork in many van Gogh paintings spilling onto the frame. Get your ears on this piece!

In May 1804 the diminutive Napoleon gave way to his considerably taller aspirations and proclaimed himself Emperor. Beethoven was furious at the news; his liberating hero was, after all, just another power-hungry 'ordinary man'. He picked up his score of the new Symphony and scratched out the 'Bonaparte' title so violently that his pen tore the paper. It was eventually published as the 'Heroic', or *Eroica* Symphony, written '… in memory of a great man'.

6. Your brother is shagging his lodger's wife's sister: I suspect there's an element of point 3 in this one. If it isn't happening for you because of life's unfeeling capriciousness, there is plenty of resentment to be harboured if it appears to be happening for someone else. There is a saying about a 'woman scorned' but in the case of Beethoven a man scorned becomes an interfering prude. When he heard in 1812 that his younger bachelor brother Johann (by now a pharmacist) was having some fun between the sheets with a similarly available woman, the composer hurried to Linz to break up the affair. He ranted to his brother, who presumably told him to mind his own business. Beethoven then went to the local bishop, the civil authorities, and finally to the police station seeking to have the woman thrown out of town. Johann settled the matter by making his mistress his wife. Stung by his brother's 'up yours', Ludwig retreated to Vienna. At this time he was writing his Eighth Symphony (1812), perhaps the most light-hearted of the series.

7. Restaurant service is lousy: What would you do if you received the wrong plate of food in a restaurant? Accept it anyway, or politely stress that it was the waiter's fault and have the dish sent back? Beethoven did neither; when he was erroneously served stewed beef in a Viennese tavern called the 'Swan' the composer picked up his dinner and tipped it over the waiter's head.

8. You dedicate yourself to bringing up your nephew and he tries to kill himself: Not content with being the brother from Hell, Beethoven proved to be similarly gifted as brother-in-law and uncle when his other brother died suddenly in 1815, leaving a nine-year-old son called Karl. Uncle Ludwig decided that he should be the child's guardian and waged a five-year legal battle with Karl's mother for sole custody, accusing her at various times of embezzlement, prostitution and theft. The welter of slander worked and the matter was finally resolved in Beethoven's favour in 1820. Here at last was the possibility of a family life that he felt had always been denied him. But a great composer can't be good at everything and in Ludwig's case one of his lesser skills was surrogate fatherhood. In 1826 nephew Karl fired two pistols at his own head in a botched suicide attempt before being returned to his mother's care.

9. The doctors keep giving you medicine when all you really need is a good drink: Even as Beethoven was exploring new musical terrain in his late series of master-pieces — the final piano sonatas, the Ninth Symphony, and the last string quartets — his external life was in increasing disarray. He moved lodgings more than forty times during his Vienna years and was the nemesis of dozens of domestic servants who fell victim to his temper and his preference for squalor; friends sometimes had to change his clothes while he slept. Under the pressure of such steam, cracks were bound to appear. And they did; Beethoven drank too much and by his early fifties his liver began to fail. He died on 26 March 1827 from cirrhosis. In his final weeks he was overjoyed when one of the attending doctors prescribed an alcoholic iced punch as a sleeping aid. Beethoven took to the medicine with such vigour that it hastened his end.

That is just a little of Beethoven's story. Like any distillation of the bad moments inside fifty-six years it is bound to make grim reading; much more so than the petty irritations we all endure and which often suffice to stop most of us in our tracks. It is natural to think that gaining speed on that distant carrot of life's purpose is impossible when so many small obstacles keep interrupting our stride. They remind us that ours is an 'ordinary' life.

But would life have felt any less 'ordinary' for Beethoven? Perhaps — but not in the sense of feeling extraordinary. There would have been stretches when the 'ordinary' would have been a comfort for him. For years at a time his output petered away to nothing when he was overwhelmed by depression or the thought-sapping minutiae of daily life — his legal wranglings over custody of his nephew, for instance. Crowning it all was his sense of being an outsider; an ostracism imposed by deafness, and probably a tremendous loneliness. Seen from the outside, he didn't cope too well. No wonder he wanted to get his hands on Fate's throat.

Every life is ordinary in the sense that we all receive low blows from the shadowy bastard across the ring, but following Beethoven's suggested tactic of going for the opponent's throat doesn't guarantee victory. His particular triumph was in continuing to punch his way *in*, using his music as a blunt instrument, forcing his way through to some personal truth. His musical sketchbooks carry the scars of the battle; much of his work didn't flow onto the page in finished form, but was chiselled out of stone through the discarding, refinement, crossing-out, reworking of ideas. If anything is superhuman about Beethoven it is this sense of effort.

We *think* we know what we want, but getting to the right solution needs agonising work. Some introspection is a useful tool here; having a good dialogue with oneself. This is the natural process of the artistic creator enacted within the mundane reality of sitting alone, converting thoughts into symbols on paper or a computer screen. Composition is a journey to the interior, asking directions on the way.

If ever you're feeling furious about life's apparent injustice you should put on the first movement of Beethoven's *Eroica* Symphony. He wrote it at a point when he had to try and accept his encroaching deafness as a likely permanent state. The symphony doesn't just start; it *detonates*. One! Two! A couple of monumental uppercuts that turn the contest around in our favour in the existential slugfest. His music abounds with these killer blows: the first movement of his *Pathétique* Piano Sonata, Op.13 (1799); the end of the *Egmont* Overture, the Ninth Symphony. You will feel positively empowered.

Losing it: Wagner said it with characteristic bluntness — 'I am not made like other people.' I'm not sure if he was referring to his genius or his standing as an artist. Certainly he became one of the archetypes of the so-called 'artistic' temperament. This excuses bad behaviour; temper tantrums, demanding one's own way, stamping of the feet. By this definition, many two-year-olds are artistic. They may be great musicians, but would you really want to know some people like these?

- The most famous maestro of all, **Arturo Toscanini** (1867–1957), achieved astonishing results through a reign of terror. For years he conducted the NBC Symphony Orchestra in the USA. The orchestra would watch in horror as his foot-stamping fits of disapproval routinely (and literally) crushed spectacles, batons and fobwatches. Eventually they gave him a watch in a solid iron casing inscribed 'For Rehearsals'.

- Toscanini once became so incensed with an unresponsive soprano that he rushed onstage, grabbed her reportedly spectacular breasts and screamed, '… if only these were brains!'

- A Toscanini Technique for Orchestral Discipline, rarely used these days, is to summon underperforming players to your dressing room after the show, line them up in a row facing the wall, and kick each of them up the backside.

- Mind you, orchestras can turn the tables. Moments before a performance, the Turin Opera Orchestra in Italy ambushed their conductor and management with a refusal to play unless fee demands were met. Calling the players' bluff, the conductor Peter Maag went onstage, explained the situation to the restive audience and declared that he would play the opera accompaniment on a piano instead. The night was a triumph and the orchestra went home in disgrace.

- The eighteenth-century Italian composer and violin virtuoso **Francesco Veracini** was considered in his day to be a little on the wild side. One day in 1722 Veracini jumped from a third-storey window in a fit of pique. The limping composer later claimed that there had been a plot against his life.

- **Maria Callas** (1923–1977) was legendary for her voice and her temper. In 1951 she attacked a Brazilian impresario with a bronze paperweight after he replaced her in a production of Puccini's *Tosca*. In Rome, in 1958, she walked out of a performance of Bellini's *Norma* after the First Act due to a rowdy reception; the President of Italy was in the audience.

- In 1945, the principal bass with the National Opera of Mexico, Ignacio Ruffino, found himself with spare time during rehearsals and decided to catch a matinée session at the local cinema. Edging his way to his seat, he noticed his wife further along looking rather too comfortable in the security of darkness with his best friend. Realising that discussion was impractical while the film was running, Ruffino pulled out his revolver and shot the man dead instead. As the perpetrator of a crime of passion, the singer was arrested but never tried. Buoyed by the sympathy of Mexican society, Ruffino continued to appear at the Opera and was happily reconciled with his wife.

Hell hath no fury…: Giacomo Puccini consistently sent his lead soprano characters to a tragic end in his operas (see **Love with Violins**) but the most tragic end of all occurred when Life imitated Art. His own romantic life would have filled many an opera plot. In 1884 he eloped with Elvira Gemignani, the wife of a merchant from the Italian Puccini's home town of Lucca. Two years later, while still his mistress, Elvira bore him a son. (Their ménage could not be legalised until the death of Elvira's husband in 1904; this was nineteenth-century Catholic Italy.)

When the success of his opera *Manon Lescaut* (yes, Manon dies at the end) brought Puccini fame and the beginning of riches in 1893, the composer began to succumb frequently to his roving eye and the temptations offered by his new celebrity. Elvira was able to 'overlook' his endless liaisons while they took place away from the Puccini *casa* at Torre del Lago. Her jealousy festered and finally erupted in 1908 when she became convinced that her husband was helping himself to their maid. In fact, Puccini and the girl were innocent — she had only been dusting his ledges — but the enraged Signora Puccini persecuted Doria Manfredi with such psychological efficiency that the younger woman committed suicide in January 1909. The ensuing court case scandalised Italy, with the complete vindication of the deceased, Puccini paying out a considerable settlement to the girl's family and the sentencing of Elvira to five months in prison.

Puccini's next opera, *The Girl of the Golden West* was premiered the following year. It is an American cowboy romance in which — unusually for the composer — the guy ends up with the girl.

***

The angry mob: As Puccini put it, 'Spectators are good people one by one. But together, once out for evil, they are rabble.' In retail the customer may always be right, but in art be wary of dealing with a shopful. If you're scared of public disapproval, or sometimes doubt your own judgement, then don't become a composer — or at least, don't insist on having your work performed.

Rossini's opera *The Barber of Seville* is one of the genre's favourite comedies. But the first performance was a disaster. Whistling and hooting drowned out the singing from the start. The composer was hissed as he sat in the orchestra pit. One of the principals accidentally fell through an open trapdoor as he sang and a cat walked across the stage during the first finale.

A staging mishap also marred the first night of Puccini's *Madam Butterfly* in 1904 at La Scala in Milan. Butterfly spun around onstage in her kimono too quickly, causing it to billow up over her head, rather like Marilyn Monroe's frock in *The Seven Year Itch*. A member of the audience yelled 'Butterfly is pregnant'. The performance continued in a welter of obscene remarks and barnyard imitations. There was no applause at the final curtain — only laughter. Puccini hid in a dressing room; afterwards, he left clutching the conductor's score to preclude a second performance at the house.

The 1913 premiere of Stravinsky's ballet *The Rite of Spring* in Paris is perhaps the most famous first-night fiasco in music. The hubbub began within seconds of opening and eventually grew to a such a pitch that the dancers on stage couldn't hear the pounding of the immense orchestra and had to follow the counting of the beat yelled from the wings, rather like a rowing team. There was much exchanging of abuse in the stalls and scuffles broke out between people armed with umbrellas. Stravinsky's supporters were just as vocal: fellow composer Florent Schmitt shouted to the stalls, 'Shut up, you bitches!' Stravinsky spent the next few weeks recovering in a nursing home.

Public opinion turned around quickly for all these works. Rossini and Puccini became very wealthy men as their operas were reappraised within weeks. Stravinsky's *Rite* is one of the iconic pieces of twentieth-century culture, period. He lived to give his autograph to Frank Sinatra and the Pope.

⋙ SADNESS ⋘

"Our sweetest songs are those that tell of
saddest thought …"
PERCY BYSSHE SHELLEY, *To a Skylark* (1820)

I'll begin with a sad tale of my own. A long time
ago I learned of the premature death of my first
love. She was French, an actor in film. We met in
Paris when I was nineteen and she eighteen. While
I was smitten to the point of irrationality, she was
merely charmed. I became a long-distance confi-
dant of her romantic and emotional travails. But not
all of them. On the eve of one of my frequent
returns to Paris to see her, she married someone
else. Her mother broke the news to me over the
phone; I remember wandering around the city in a
stupor for days. She had a child, the marriage broke
down. One day she checked in to a five-star hotel
and committed suicide. She was twenty-six.

I DIDN'T RECEIVE the news until four years later. Shock is always immediate — erasing feeling, paralysing comprehension — but people then begin to engage their grief at different speeds. In my case, years had gone by. I was sitting alone in a cafe in Paris in a touristy pocket where the Boulevard St Michel hits the Seine; Notre Dame Cathedral is literally just over your shoulder. There was nothing around me conducive to melancholy on a golden spring afternoon with crowds of people swirling around a kerbside accordionist squeezing out his small repertoire of Parisian musical clichés.

I don't remember the precise moment of impact during this melancholy serenade. It certainly proved Noël Coward's line in his play *Private Lives* about the potency of 'cheap music'. Suddenly I was aware of that awful prickling behind the eyes and thanked heaven for the cover of my sunglasses as the first real wave of recollection and sorrow swept by. One of those inconspicuous tunes had fired off a symphony of loss in my memory; loss of time, youth, opportunity, love — the usual self-pitying grievances. I was miserable in Paris all over again, and a part of me loved it. The purge took several hours, two more beers, and a change of busker. Weeping tourists must be as commonplace as Gallic reserve in that part of the world because I was spared any solicitations. He weeps happiest who weeps alone.

People like Oscar Wilde and Stravinsky have insisted that music doesn't represent anything. It follows that, being essentially abstract, music's capacity to incite emotion is reliant on the susceptibility of the listener. In other words, the more one is moved, the more one is a sucker. Two hundred years ago the English politician and journalist William Cobbett stated that '… a great fondness for music is a mark of great weakness and great vacuity of mind'. This is naturally a disconcerting accusation for someone like me whose strongest response to music remains an emotional one.

But whether music 'finds' the emotion or vice versa is difficult to say. Despite some of the recommendations in this book there remains the distressing probability that no single piece of music is guaranteed to make you happy. This is evidenced by the expressions on the faces of orchestral conductors who, after all, know what is coming and never look too pleased about it.

Can music, then, make you sad? I suppose that depends on one's vulnerability at the time: for instance, I haven't wept at the sound of an accordion since my Parisian episode (although I can still wince at a concertina). The jury has been out on this for centuries, ranging from Cervantes ('he who sings scares away his woes …', *Don Quixote*) to Shakespeare ('I am never merry when I hear sweet music …', *The Merchant of Venice*). Music has certainly been more than happy to *articulate* sadness in all its forms; melancholy, grief, regret, self-loathing and so on. The tapestry of music has many black threads.

One would imagine that composers have the misery-peddling franchise all to themselves. In truth, they're about as unhappy as the rest of us; they just look miserable because smiling was the first casualty of poor dental hygiene (although twentieth-century composers aren't grinners, come to think of it). There are exceptions: composers who were wired for both a lifetime and an oeuvre of sadness. One of the flag-bearers of this tragic troupe is Peter (or to be more Russian about it) **Peter Ilyich Tchaikovsky** (1840–1893).

> *"Fate … hangs perpetually over our heads and is always embittering the soul."*
> PETER ILYICH TCHAIKOVSKY, 1878

The world loves Tchaikovsky. I love him; and so — probably — do you. In his own day he was also popular, even lionised. But this eventual celebrity and official recognition didn't help him a whit. He was miserable; full of self-loathing, doubts about his work, and an always darkening pessimism about life's transience. His music often displays a grandiose sense of tragedy, even when it is in a major key. Listen to the opening of the Pas de deux from his ballet *The Nutcracker* (1892); really just a descending major scale. It's slow, but it should feel happy — church bells sound the same thing as a celebratory peal. In Tchaikovsky's hands the effect is quite the opposite, and the melody moves on with obvious relief to the related minor key. The opening of the glorious Serenade for Strings (1880) is similarly resplendent but again just a little uncomfortable about it. The pretence of happiness never lasts long. The list of his works includes an early symphonic poem called *Fate*; a *Sérénade mélancolique* (1875); and his final composition, the *Pathétique* Symphony (1893) which has — yes — the saddest, most mournful and pessimistic ending of any major example of the genre. Soon after this Symphony's premiere in 1893, Tchaikovsky committed suicide.

And yet the beauty of the music proves Shelley's poetic dictum quoted above. What gets us about Peter? Simply this: his are some of the 'sweetest songs' ever written. Tchaikovsky had the knack of having the right tune at the right time. He could even come up with the right tune at the wrong time, such as in the opening of his Piano Concerto No.1, in which that immortal melody is intoned by the orchestra over crashing piano chords only to be promptly discarded and never referred to again. A brain has to be crammed with ideas to come up with a whopper like that and then just move on because there is so much more to do.

Tchaikovsky often felt compelled by a sense of urgency, of racing against the clock. Even in his mid-forties he would write of life's brevity, of things yet to be accomplished: 'We keep putting things off and meanwhile death lurks round the corner.' A real, if not delightful, prospect. Tchaikovsky was right.

This was in large part the haste of the late starter. Tchaikovsky was hardly born to music: his father was a successful mining engineer and 'creative artist' was hardly the occupation of choice for sons of good middle-class families in mid-nineteenth-century Russia. Sure, young Peter would tinker for hours on the family orchestrion (a sort of domestic calliope, the bells and whistles contraption that serenades merry-go-rounds) and he complained about the difficulty of removing music lodged in his head — but every sensitive young kid has fancies.

As things turned out, Tchaikovsky didn't begin serious theoretical study of music until he was twenty-one. Even Berlioz didn't leave it this late. I always read this single fact with considerable relief, still clinging to the hope that it is never too late to discover the path to one's bliss. Career decisions have an unfortunate habit of taking one's eye off the main game.

Not that the future composer's life had been uneventful up to this point. A calm childhood in the provinces was interrupted in 1848 when Tchaikovsky *père* dragged everyone to the big smoke of St Petersburg to pursue a job offer that proved illusory; Peter's beloved governess Fanny Dürbach was retrenched in the process. Unhappy schooldays and a six-month rest spell with measles followed. In 1854 the emotionally fragile teenager was shattered by the death of his mother from cholera. Music was his consolation; improvising at the piano and making a few stabs at writing with his still rudimentary technical knowledge. After leaving school in 1859 (where his grades had been ordinary) Tchaikovsky became a clerk in the Ministry of Justice, staying there for four years and being the dandy young man around town after hours until full-time music study took over.

It was a long time coming, but when Tchaikovsky eventually found his purpose an immense and long-dormant creative faculty was activated. This was a man who worried constantly about having enough time left to empty the contents of a mind seething with ideas. Two years after taking up music study full-time he was already teaching harmony at the new Moscow Conservatoire. By 1869 he'd written his first masterpiece, the *Romeo and Juliet* Fantasy Overture (complete with one of the great love themes), spurring him into the 1870s and works like the *Marche Slave*, the First Piano Concerto, the Violin Concerto, the Fourth Symphony, his first ballet *Swan Lake*, and the opera *Eugene Onegin*. The musical tap was running.

Meanwhile, other pressures were building. Tchaikovsky was gay, and the ensuing struggle with his sexuality was the great drama of his life. In his time in Russia, homosexuality was an offence punishable by exile to Siberia, but the composer's efforts to suppress this part of himself would appear to have been driven by more complex causes than a mere fear of suspicion, or worse, conviction; there were always opportunities in big cities like St Petersburg and Moscow, after all. He was a captive of the prevailing morality of the time and felt tremendous guilt about his 'inclinations' which he described as both 'natural' and '... the greatest obstacle to happiness'.

Tchaikovsky's attempted solution in 1877 was desperate and naive in the extreme. Declaring that marriage would silence rumours about him, he proceeded to wed a plainly unstable young woman who had written him a love letter in 1877, threatening suicide if he would not see her, and to whom he proposed within a week of their first meeting, knowing full well that a physical relationship would be impossible.

Oh, Peter — you idiot. He probably said the same early on their honeymoon night on the train from Moscow to St Petersburg. (Ken Russell's film about Tchaikovsky, *The Music Lovers*, offers a graphic representation of the naked and optimistic Mrs Tchaikovsky rolling around the floor of their compartment. While in reality the composer was 'on the point of screaming', his wife stayed obligingly clothed and upright.) The arrangement was an instant catastrophe. Tchaikovsky was on the verge of complete breakdown within days. This was July 1877; in early October he tried to induce pneumonia by walking into the freezing Moskva River. He fled Moscow days later to suffer a complete nervous collapse while under the care of one of his younger brothers. Doctors recommended that he never see his wife again. This astute prescription initiated a swift recovery.

The former Mrs Tchaikovsky was certified as insane in 1896 and died in an asylum in 1917.

Concurrent with Tchaikovsky's marital fiasco ran another relationship with a woman that maintained a higher degree of candour and emotional intimacy than found in many marriages. It was conducted entirely by mail with one Nadezhda von Meck, the wealthy widow of a railway magnate. Her admiration for the composer had more than a touch of love in it and was manifested by a generous annuity that helped to keep him afloat financially for fourteen years (1876–1890) and partially subsidised the writing of great works like the Fourth (dedicated to her) and Fifth Symphonies, the Serenade for Strings and the *Capriccio Italien* (1880). She was his long-distance shoulder to cry on — meaning that her shoulder was perpetually moist — and invisible hostess at several estates where Tchaikovsky could work and weep alone, rent-free. Apart from accidental sightings on two occasions, the pair never met.

Tchaikovsky was depressed about the end of each passing day and kept a number of diaries as a way of making a souvenir of time. He then became anxious about others reading their contents and ensured most of them were destroyed.

The composer was restless when at home and homesick while he was away. In the years immediately after his failed marriage he travelled extensively around Europe with generous financial assistance from supporters at the Russian Musical Society, from his benefactress Nadezhda von Meck, and eventually from the Tsar himself. He was free to compose full-time but this liberty brought him little joy because of his ruthless self-criticism: 'I have achieved nothing', he would write, '… am I played out?' For many years alcohol was his comfort.

Concert tours took him as far afield as the United States, where he conducted the opening concerts at Carnegie Hall in 1891. (He had become more secure on the podium since his first-ever appearance in 1868, when he was terrified that his head would fall off.) Tchaikovsky's sister died before the tour began and the devastated composer spent his first night in New York weeping in his hotel room.

⟨※⟩

His constant depressions made him hypochondriacal and he complained of insomnia, 'apoplectic strokes', migraines and various aches and pains. 'You cannot imagine anyone who suffers more than I do', he wrote to his brother Modest in 1874. He would assert that the compulsion to feign illness was as much an illness as any actual physical infirmity.

⟨※⟩

We shouldn't imagine that Tchaikovsky composed by shedding copious tears on a blank page and having them blossom into crotchets. The dialogue with himself achieved by writing music gave him his greatest happiness. Indeed, one lesson to draw from the lives of these composers is that *creative hard work can be therapeutic.* Sure, these artists may have been a bit AWOL once the pen, the brush or the chisel was put down — the odd fired pistol, sliced ear or (in Tchaikovsky's case) spilled vodka — but the process of organising and notating thought in a work as complex as, say, his *Pathétique* Symphony requires absolute clarity of mind. You can't meander drunkenly through a fugue.

This last symphony of Tchaikovsky is a good example. He was in appalling spirits before starting the work in February 1893, writing that 'my faith in myself is shattered, and my role is ended'. Then the engine turned over; three weeks later, he had already sketched out the complete first movement on paper with the rest of the piece ready in his head. He realised he still had the ticker. The music collapses with grief at the end, yet it was composed on a high. Tchaikovsky was uncharacteristically upbeat about its quality, declaring the Symphony his best and 'most sincere' work. Even the lukewarm reception from the audience and the critics at its premiere in St Petersburg on 28 October 1893 didn't faze him.

Nine days later he was dead.

Now this is a really sad story. For many years we were all told that Tchaikovsky's death was caused by drinking unboiled water during a cholera epidemic. Whether it was accidental or not was unclear, but there was greater poetry in thinking that the *Pathétique* Symphony was a musical suicide note.

Another story has emerged only in recent years with an even more (dare I say it) pathetic scenario. Tchaikovsky was going to be 'outed' by a member of the Russian aristocracy in a letter to the Tsar accusing the composer of shenanigans with the complainant's nephew. The letter's emissary, an 'old boy' of the School of Jurisprudence that Tchaikovsky had attended in the 1850s, was disturbed at the disgrace this would bring upon the institution. A strange meeting of other 'old boys' was convened with the composer present. The verdict of this strange jury was that the school's honour must be preserved by his immediate suicide. Arsenic did the job.

FEELING LOW?
Try These Sure-Fire
Tchaikovsky ANTI-DEPRESSANTS!!

Things look grim at the end of the Sixth Symphony (*Pathétique*) Op.74 but there's help nearby. Just go to the penultimate (third) movement of the same work: a roof-raising march. Go get 'em, it roars.

You'll be on your feet and hooting for more after the finale to the Violin Concerto, Op.35. This one's a fighter — its dedicatee declared it impossible to play in 1878 and the reviews were hardly more complimentary after its 1881 premiere — 'music that stinks to the ear,' said one. She's come up roses ever since. Beautiful all the way through, but turn the volume up in the third movement.

When I think back to the one piece that finally hooked me into classical music as a child it would have to be *The Nutcracker* Suite, Op.71a, drawn from the ballet completed in 1892. What an orchestral genius Tchaikovsky was! Even before seeing the animated realisation of the music in Walt Disney's *Fantasia* I had given it a thorough belting on the family radiogram, conjuring up my own mental pictures to moments like the Arabian Dance and the Waltz of the Flowers. Thirty-five years later I was conducting that same waltz with the Tasmanian Symphony Orchestra and almost had to recompose myself after the very first play through at rehearsal. Poor Peter. For him it may have been a lousy life, but I'm grateful he was around. The rest of the ballet is just as good, by the way, as are his two earlier ballets *Swan Lake* (1877) and *The Sleeping Beauty* (1890).

***

Happiness is life's soufflé but sadness is somehow more interesting. We love to probe through something that is dark and suppurating, singling out the layers for inspection. Music also likes to plumb these depths and we often feel that in doing so it is edging towards some sort of ultimate truth. The minor scale with its flattened third in the scale promises a darker, more spiritual sound world than the ostensibly 'happier' major scale. Imagine the opening of Mozart's Symphony No.40 played in G major, rather than G minor; it would sound almost twee. If, at the end of a symphony, the early miserable 'minor' theme is given a 'major' reincarnation, it denotes a triumphant passage into the light, but it also suggests the interesting times of working things out are over.

In opera, characters only reveal their complexity when they are miserable; a happy diva has less to sing about than one who is contemplating suicide or purdah (see Puccini's heroines in **Love with Violins**). Dido, the Queen of ancient Carthage, sounds pleased when she's being courted by Aeneas in Purcell's *Dido and Aeneas* (c1689) and Berlioz's *The Trojans* (1863), but it is only after he has dumped her to take an early package tour to Italy that her music becomes truly great; she is literally dying with grief. Unalloyed happiness in opera is usually given to the chorus at the beginning of Act One (or in tavern scenes and tableaux of simple village life), to the local idiot, or to those in positions of subservience; it has been a social and political tenet for centuries that the lower classes don't have the capacity or the right to be unhappy.

Sadness in music almost always involves the loss of something once possessed rather than frustrated ambition. There aren't too many operas and symphonies about failing to get a promotion. Lost love is obviously a hot favourite but loss of youth and innocence is also high in the rankings.

❧

Edward Elgar was deeply affected by loss, subsuming it into a nostalgia for a vanishing world, the disappearance of a way of life. There is not a great deal we can do about the 'things aren't what they used to be' misery: hide from a changing world, or continue to go with the flow. But a man who at sixty-four could describe himself as 'still at heart a dreamy child' was not one to embrace life's future possibilities. Even in his mid-forties, when life and career were on the up, Elgar was nostalgic about his childhood, writing two little pieces for small orchestra called *Dream Children* (1902) inspired by an essay of Charles Lamb's that concludes: 'We are nothing; less than nothing, and dreams. We are only what might have been.' And this from a composer with the *Enigma Variations* (1899), the song cycle *Sea Pictures* (1899), and the oratorio *The Dream of Gerontius* (1900) — three masterpieces within three years — just behind him!

Elgar was able to capture the national mood of late Victorian and Edwardian England; the opulence, the occasionally blustering pride, the beating of the national heart beneath the corsetted breast. And when it went, Elgar missed it. His post-War works have a valedictory quality, like the magnificent Cello Concerto of 1919. When his much-loved wife Alice died in 1920 most of his creative urge went with her. He composed almost nothing more and retreated to the countryside, consoling himself with trips to the races. On his deathbed, he muttered a short remark about himself to a friend that will always remain a secret; '… only five words,' said the friend, 'but they are too tragic for the ear of the mob.' What possible phrase could be so devastating? Sadness may well be the key to unlocking character but one should throw it away when closing the door for the last time.

Franz Schubert writes like an old friend; the pudgy scholarly guy in the corner who murmurs words of wisdom in an undertone. I'm tempted to describe him as a sad figure purely on the basis of his short lifespan. We often fancy that those who are to die young have some subliminal premonition that makes them write at speed in the meantime. What tripe. Schubert gushed, rather than composed, hundreds of songs onto paper in his thirty-one years and would have gushed hundreds more with a few more decades under his belt.

Schubert's friends adored him. He played great piano at parties. And yet for all these Viennese good times there is a twilight in much of his music, a sense of transience, and a real knowledge of the agony of love and the pain of rejection. The mournful narrator of the song cycle *The Fair Maid of the Mill* (1823) experiences all the emotions outlined in this book in the course of an unrequited love, but his Peace comes only when he drowns himself. The cycle is a symbol of Schubert's own inner turmoil of the time; in 1822 he contracted syphilis from a prostitute, and much of the song cycle was written while he was in hospital receiving the ghastly mercury treatments, causing him to lose some of his hair. It is heart-rending to read a letter by a young man who writes: '… I feel myself to be the most unhappy and wretched creature in the world … on retiring to bed, I hope I may not wake again' (1824). But Schubert is a hero, like all of our cast, and he pushed on — if not with the confidence of before.

The sorrow of parting: Schubert was prey to self-blame but **Gustav Mahler's** (1860-1911) fatalism encompasses Life and the World. Perhaps he was predisposed to such a philosophy; even as a kid he declared that his life ambition was to be a martyr. Much later, as a patient of Sigmund Freud, he recalled that he once ran terrified from his childhood home during a violent argument between his parents, only to hurtle into a street hurdy-gurdy grinding out a Viennese popular song. The memory of this juxtaposition of banality and pain never left him and it's this blend of irony and despair that has seen such a renaissance of Mahler's reputation since the end of the Second World War.

A Mahler symphony is a trip that takes up most of a concert (there are nine, plus a tenth completed by someone else). One can't help feeling like a psychiatrist while listening to it as Gustav spills the beans from the couch. Even if you're into his confessions, a thermos with warm brandy provides useful sustenance — keep it under your concert hall seat for a generous swig between movements and don't show it to the usherette.

To be fair, Life did give him a kick in the guts when his adored eldest daughter died of scarlet fever in 1907 and he was also diagnosed with a life-threatening heart problem. He was truly afflicted with goodbyes. That same year he began his setting of texts based on ancient Chinese poetry, a virtual symphony with solo voices. Initially called 'The Song of Earthly Sorrow', it became *The Song of the Earth*. It is an ocean of Mahler's life philosophy, one feels: in the opening 'Drinking Song of Earth's Misery' the key phrase is 'Dark is life, dark is death'. Despite the old Eastern origins, we don't get musical haiku. The setting of the final poem, 'The Farewell' (*Der Abschied*), takes nearly half an hour. I'm not one for long goodbyes, but this is no mere tear-stained waving on the dock. It makes sadness feel like a privilege.

⇢⊙ FREEDOM & RELEASE ⊙⇠

"A man of superior talents becomes bad if he always stays in the same place."
WOLFGANG AMADEUS MOZART, 1778

Profession: *Musician-Philosopher*
Coming from: *Doubt*
Journeying towards: *Truth*
FRANZ LISZT, Entry in a hotel register, 1836

A time for action: You've finally had enough and want to set yourself free. One snip and that unsatisfactory relationship or stultifying job could be cut away, like tired but still over-tight suspenders. The lure is overwhelming; an ensuing lightness of spirit, the freedom of travel, the luxury of entertaining new options. Why, then, is this simple action of release so difficult for most of us? A lack of courage, a strong attachment to routine, or an over-developed sense of responsibility?

WE WOULD ALWAYS plump for the latter. You and I are reliable people, after all: not like those 'artistic' types. Composers seem such creatures of whim, such enthusiastic tourists in theme parks of their own creation; they had no compunction about upping sticks and hustling on to the next city where an audience awaited. Travelling minstrels, most of them.

Of course, we are wrong about ourselves and our cast. The truth is always so much more mundane. For hundreds of years composers and performers were considered to be mere crotchet-bearing providores. In palaces and mansions the sonatas were delivered at the back door along with the cabbages. Even Mozart was a lowly-paid servant for the early part of his career, joining a profession who were captives of drudgery ('... a concerto — tomorrow? Of course, your Majesty'). Most of them would have loved to pull out the scissors. But a man without suspenders has his pants on the floor.

<hr>

Snip snip: Mozart was one of classical music's free spirits. In 1781, he abruptly broke his service with the Archbishop of Salzburg — employment with a wealthy patron which was as much as musicians of his day could hope for. Being made to sit at a table below even the valets when travelling with the royal entourage ('at least I have the honour of sitting ahead of the cooks'), as well as the miserable salary, had finally exasperated his sense of self-worth. He also had a head full of music which was not about to be emptied in the course of his employment for a phlegmatic member of the Church.

'Breaking his service' is perhaps a genteel way of putting it. In fact, Mozart's resignation was sealed with 'a kick on my arse by order of our worthy Prince Archbishop'. It was classical music's most fateful boot up the behind, propelling Mozart into a new world, a rarely visited world for a musician in those days … that of the freelance musician — the 'gun for hire'. He had cut the suspenders. Now he just had to keep his pants up.

Mozart was twenty-five and already beginning the final decade of his life which thereafter darkened steadily as he worked himself into an early — and unmarked — grave.

Several years ago I began radio broadcasting on a daily basis, playing classical music to listeners at that most vulnerable time of the early morning. Loving the music as I do, I tended to enthuse volubly about it by trying to explain my own reactions. This subjective approach polarised my new audience for a while. Some thought this inappropriate for great music. To them I was just a vandal spraying graffiti on the walls of these temples of perfection. I was taken aback by such criticism. My intention had been simply to open a few doors.

There was a marvellous letter of complaint in a Melbourne newspaper which listed various transgressions, the most grave being my presentation of Mozart. In talking about the young Salzburg genius, she said, I had resorted to 'coarse and vulgar expressions'. (In truth, there may have been a bottom joke.) 'Get that girl off the air!' was the concluding war-cry.

I took great pleasure in replying to the aggrieved matron that the offending words of the introduction in question had fortunately not been mine; in fact, I had been quoting from one of Mozart's own letters. The vulgarian had been the composer himself.

Wolfgang Amadeus Mozart (1756–1791) was an astonishing talent. He was possibly the most naturally and abundantly gifted musician the Western world has ever known. Some time ago a number of psychologists were asked to try and estimate the IQs of some of history's great creators. Some of the results were astronomically high — I think that Goethe and Michelangelo clocked in at over two hundred apiece — but in the case of Mozart they wouldn't even hazard a punt.

No wonder people were both curious and slack-jawed back in the 1760s when the child Mozart was touring Europe with his father and older sister. The raw figures on his precocity are amazing:

170

- Mozart was picking out tunes at the keyboard at three and demonstrating perfect pitch at four when telling his elders that their violins were a quarter-tone out of tune. (That's half of a semitone we can play on the piano.)
- At five he had become a keyboard virtuoso, at six he was being relentlessly exhibited around Europe by his father Leopold, playing in royal courts and musical academies as well as to the public.
- At seven he picked up a violin and played it — even though he'd had no violin lessons.
- At eight he wrote his Symphony No.1 in E flat, K.16.

His first major opera, *La finta semplice*, premiered when he was thirteen and from then on Mozart's output was staggeringly prolific as you can see if you scan the Köchel catalogue of his music first compiled in the 1860s — well over six hundred works. In fact, it has been estimated that a music copyist working by hand would be hard pressed to write as many notes in the same time.

Mozart worked fast, and he was talented enough to take shortcuts; for instance, he could think out a complete string quartet and write out the individual parts *first* before making the full score, or he could notate a complicated piece on paper while thinking out another piece in his head. (See his amazing feat of transcription with Allegri's *Miserere* in **Hope**.)

There are plenty of stories like these, and when hearing them you just have to give up trying to understand how such a mind can work. Because these are the more obvious acrobatic dimensions of the talent; the real miracle lies in the quality of the work itself, not in these child prodigy days, but in the all-too-short adult phase of his life.

It's estimated that Mozart was 'on the road', so to speak, for about fourteen of his thirty-five years, meaning that he was exposed to all of the stylistic currents in European music-making; a real patchwork quilt of influences to choose from. Mozart's intellect was easily able to absorb and master all of them, but pulling out the thread of one's own voice can be difficult when the tapestry is so large, even for a genius.

Even for Mozart, you have to look to his mid-twenties before his real musical self emerges. Once that's clarified, of course, the stream of masterpieces is overwhelming, and certainly proved so to many of his contemporaries. There is the famous testimony by the elder statesman of composers, **Joseph Haydn** (1732–1809), to Mozart's father in 1785: 'I tell you before God, as an honest man, your son is the greatest composer known to me in person and by name.'

This was praise indeed for a musician not yet thirty. Haydn, after all, was no slouch himself. But the older man was perceptive; Mozart had tested and mastered every form of instrumental and vocal music. Make any generic list you like and he'll be up there somewhere. Symphonies? His last three (numbers 39-41) were composed in about six weeks with no prospect of imminent performance; he never lived to hear them 'in the flesh'. We have made up for it since then; they're still among the most-played symphonies in the world. The first movement of Symphony No.40 in G minor, K.550 became a bizarre disco hit in the 1970s, barely surviving the superimposition of a drum-kit. The finale to the Symphony No.41 in C, K.551 (nicknamed 'Jupiter') is the culmination of Mozart's late interest in fugue and counterpoint; the themes slip around each other like a ringful of mud-wrestlers. The sense of physicality almost overwhelms the listener by the closing bars.

Concertos appealed to Mozart's creative personality with their symbolism of solo instrument(s) breaking free from the webbing of orchestral accompaniment. My first hearing of a Mozart concerto was that for Flute and Harp, K.299 — or K.297c, depending on the date of the Köchel catalogue (1778); the combination is so attractive in sound that I'm surprised more concertos weren't written for the duo. (Wolfgang sets a beautifully daunting precedent, however.) Many of the keyboard concertos — he wrote twenty-seven — were 'make-work' exercises for the diminutive composer/virtuoso hungry for performance fees. Solo status apart, Mozart doesn't necessarily allow the piano to have all the fun; the opening of the Concerto No.27, K.595 (1791) — his last — allocates a profusion of melodies to the orchestra at the start. They just keep coming. Lesser composers would trade in their wooden dentures for just one tune in this league, but here's the Austrian handing them out like campaign leaflets.

The middle movement of the Piano Concerto No.21,

K.467 (1785) has of course become famous as the quintessential art-film soundtrack; its opening theme traced high in Wedgwood blue over a gently-throbbing accompaniment. This is what is meant by pure Rococo 'prettiness', one assumes. And yet there is something else in there; shadows thrown into the music by something just beyond our field of perception.

<hr />

There is darkness in every personality and it's hardly revelatory to suggest that in Mozart's case some of this stems from the relationship with his father Leopold. I'm not going to try and be Freudian here, but one doesn't have to be too astute to realise that such a childhood — the rootlessness, transitory friendships, endless praise from strangers, continuous demands from an exploitative father — isn't perhaps the best preparation for a responsible adult life.

Mozart was a good son but his dad was a nag. Get a good job and keep it was Leopold's mantra; don't mix with unsavoury people. Look after your money and respect it. Sound familiar? Of course it does; it's the advice that most parents give to their children. Wolfgang was never about to become a delinquent but he was headstrong and the temperamental opposite of his father. Moreover, he was a free-spirited genius, and as such was virtually predestined to let the conservative Leopold down.

The free spirit reaches an apotheosis in Mozart's operas. He thought of himself as '… a composer who understands the stage'. More than this: he understood people, and he shows us real three-dimensional beings in all their complexity and subtlety for almost the first time in opera. They either chafe inside a system — as does the wily but good-hearted Figaro in *The Marriage of Figaro*, anything but blindly subservient to his employer — or they break free and go exploring for sexual conquest on a statistical scale (*Don Giovanni* — see **Lust**), the limits of fidelity (*Così fan tutte* — see **Some Musical Life Tips**), or wisdom (*The Magic Flute*, which also contains Mozart's idea of the parent from hell in the character of The Queen of the Night). For Mozart, it seems, the truly free spirit is one that can accept human frailties; his characters forgive each other their misdirected desires, and at the end of *Così* even beg the indulgence of the audience. It is the aristocratic libertine Don Giovanni whose refusal to change his point of view sees his spirit cast into an infernal cage.

Did I say 'release' at the start of this chapter? How apt. There was a kind of release that gave Mozart a hearty laugh all his life, and it involved toilet humour. The 'whoopsie' and all its warning signs are a recurring motif in his jokes with his family — and in theirs too, it should be noted. In part this was an element of the kid that never grew up (don't most children get a giggle from a fart?), but it was also a product of his domestic and cultural environment. Salzburgers were noted in the 1770s as being '… exceedingly inclined to low humour'. For some spicy, if less than fragrant reading, try to find a volume of his letters. Mozart was positively entranced by the activities of his rear end but I don't intend (if you'll pardon me saying so) to go into it here.

Freedom doesn't always work: Casting your fate to the winds sounds romantic, but it helps to be a little sensible when it comes to the world's mundane matters; you know, paying the rent and practising the odd bit of strategic diplomacy. Both are tall orders if you've been brought up as a child prodigy; the expectation is that someone else will take care of such loose ends.

One of the false Mozart legends is that fate and a jealous circle of enemies deprived him of both money and opportunity. It's true that Mozart didn't have much luck with landlords — in fact, he moved house eleven times in his last nine years — and he had to beg more than a few florins from friends in the last years of his life. But it's not that Mozart didn't have money coming in. Even when on his uppers, Mozart still kept servants, stabled a horse in the Vienna Woods for riding every afternoon, and frequently indulged in new clothes — his fellow composer Muzio Clementi remarked that Mozart dressed 'like an aristocratic courtier'. We now know that Mozart earned more than most musicians around him, and far more than he could ever have expected to earn back in Salzburg.

So what happened to the money? Mozart wasn't a heavy drinker or a gambler; nevertheless, no sooner did the money come in, and large gobs of it at that, than it was gone, and the detectives among modern musicologists are still trying to trace where. Yes, Mozart could lend to unreliable friends indiscriminately; yes, his wife Constanze was a frequent visitor to some of the fashionable and expensive health resorts to take the waters. But we've still a way to go.

And then there's the greatest mystery — still, after all these years — Mozart's sudden and dramatic death. Early nineteenth century gossip claimed murder by poison as the cause, with the likeliest perpetrator being Mozart's rival composer **Antonio Salieri** (1750-1825). By 1824 the audience at a performance of Beethoven's Ninth Symphony was being handed leaflets describing Salieri standing by Mozart's side with a poisoned cup. Two years later the Russian Pushkin enshrined the rumour in a 'dramatic dialogue', *Mozart and Salieri,* which Rimsky-Korsakov later turned into an opera. And of course we have the play *Amadeus* by Peter Shaffer that was adapted for the screen with enormous success in 1984.

So young! so young! we all cry these days — but dying at thirty-five really wasn't all that unusual in Mozart's time.

Neither was he buried in a pauper's grave, but in a simple unmarked one, as was the lot of most people. It wasn't raining at Mozart's funeral, as the 1984 film *Amadeus* tried to convince us, and as would befit the tragedy of neglected genius; we've found the weather reports from those days and discovered it was quite a pleasant early winter's day. The wrongfully accused Salieri not only followed Mozart's coffin to its resting place on 7 December 1791, he also became the music teacher for Mozart's son Franz Xaver Wolfgang. This didn't seem to bother Mozart's widow.

One of the world authorities on Mozart's medical history happens to be a stomach specialist who lives in Melbourne, Dr Peter Davies. Mozart was never a particularly robust specimen, and Dr Davies theorises with persuasive evidence that the composer fell victim to a recurrent and in those days very common streptococcal infection that caused flu symptoms the first time around, and complete renal failure the second, with anything up to ten years separating the two illnesses. It was a nasty European version of the 'flu'; a shot of penicillin would probably have saved him. We are left with music's greatest 'what if': imagine what he would have done with another thirty-five years. At least we have the *first* thirty-five.

An older free spirit: Clément Janequin (c1485–1558) also found himself outside the system back in the days when a regular position in a cathedral or court was *de rigueur*. Early employers kept dying on him and a series of prebends were short-lived and low-paid (Janequin studied for the priesthood). In any case, masses and motets weren't his 'thing'; he preferred writing secular songs — or, as they call them in France, chansons. Their subjects ranged from love to battle, and they were full of effects: animal impressions, sighs of love, war cries and the sounds of the elements.

This early musical free spirit was only ever employed sporadically. In his early sixties he enrolled at the Paris University as a mature-age student, perhaps to fatten up his educational qualifications for those upcoming job interviews. It was all to no avail. Janequin left little at his death, and what there was went to charity, rather than to his family. He had never held an important regular position. Today his chansons are sung more widely than ever, but modern-day concert hall settings would have amazed Janequin. He was never happier than when belting out his own tunes in three or four parts with friends around a table.

Travel and transcendence: How free-ranging this sounds — a young, long-haired Hungarian-born piano virtuoso elopes from Paris to Switzerland in 1835 with another man's wife. She bears him three children while he further refines an already astonishing keyboard technique and writes music in lakeside villas scented with magnolias. This is a fragment of the picturesque (and picaresque) life of **Franz Liszt** (1811–1886), who would quite easily have filled every chapter of this little book. The woman was the Countess Marie d'Agoult; the pair and an occasional retinue of bohemians caused a stir in hotel lobbies everywhere (see Liszt's entry in a register at the top of this chapter). This really does seem like freedom: a relationship outside conventional morality pursued in isolated snow-capped surroundings, evening reveries in a gondola, and a disdain for possessions. Marie wrote: '... a bad piano, a few books, the conversation of a serious-minded woman suffice for him.' Later, in Switzerland, Liszt began to write his collections of pieces called *Years of Pilgrimage*.

Too good to last? That's right — despite all this 'freedom' Marie suffered spells of depression and wrote gloomily: 'I feel myself an obstacle to his life.' The relationship soured. Liszt embarked on another type of 'freedom' by inventing the modern piano recital and playing concerts all over Europe over a period of nine years from 1838: from Moscow to Lisbon, Constantinople to Belfast — more than a thousand concerts in all. These were the years of so-called 'Lisztomania' (see **Lust**).

Eventually this life on the road lost its lustre for Liszt. He said, '... always concerts! Always to be a valet of the public! What a trade!' In 1847 he announced his intention of retiring from the concert platform for good and never again played in public for his own benefit. He was going to settle down, with a new love, of course. He was thirty-five years old.

Freedom is relative.

An even bigger tearaway was the Spaniard **Isaac Albéniz** (1860–1909). Initially self-taught at the piano, he made his debut in Barcelona when aged four. At seven he was taken to Paris but came a cropper when caught breaking the windows in his classroom. Back in Spain, he started running away from home, eventually stowing away on a boat to South America, living by his wits and talents all over the continent. He was not yet a teenager. Back in Europe, he finished his piano studies with Franz Liszt. That classic 'Spanish' sound in piano music owes much to Albéniz.

Wandering in music: The concept of 'the journey' contains many spiritual and metaphysical resonances; the journey is us, going through life. 'A stranger I came, a stranger I depart' is the opening phrase of Franz Schubert's late song cycle *Winter's Journey* (1827). The cold starkness of the settings reflect inner and outer landscapes. Berlioz's symphony *Harold in Italy* (1834) tracks our Byronic hero's encounters with bandits, lovers and pilgrims while referring to his inner turmoil. It's an early example of travel's opportunity for introspection.

This may be one of the reasons why pilgrimages were undertaken in such volume during the Middle Ages. People would leave their homes around Europe to trek to such places as Santiago de Compostela in Spain, braving weather, ill-health and bandits, never certain that they would see their loved ones again. Friendly monasteries would put the travellers up en route. One of them, the shrine of Montserrat near Barcelona, had its monks knock out some tunes for the pilgrims' entertainment before lights out — they were often in high spirits, we're told. Some of the music was collected in a fourteenth-century volume that we call *Llibre Vermell*, the 'Red Book' of Montserrat. Seven hundred years later, the melodies still hypnotise, taking us inside the mind and mood of the medieval pilgrim.

A modern pilgrim's tale: Regular listeners to my radio programmes were right to discern a sympathy for Celtic and medieval music. Perhaps I was a Gaelic-crooning penitent in a former life; certainly I experienced déjà vu several years ago when a particularly late-night Irish sounding piece with the characteristic sound of whistles, pipes and harps turned out to be from Spain; from Galicia in fact, in its northwestern corner, invaded by the Celts in about 800 BC and then by the Romans (who left behind the name) some six hundred years later. One morning a listener phoned to tell me about her son's wedding to a Galician local, the wedding party serenaded by pipe bands as they processed along rolling green hills. I became increasingly fascinated by this superimposition of cultures in what

I thought was one of the least visited parts of Europe.

It turns out that Galicia has been a major tourist destination for more than a thousand years; ever since word was enthusiastically leaked out that the remains of Saint James, one of the original band of Christ's disciples, had been discovered by a local bishop on a remote hillside in the area after some divine constellational finger-pointing. From this seed — or more appropriately, those bones — sprang the church, then the monastery, then the city of Santiago de Compostela, destination for countless medieval pilgrims from all over Europe. One of them, a French cleric called Aimeric Picaud, documented the main route through Spain in his *Codex Calixtinus* in the mid-twelfth century; probably the first real travel guide.

Pilgrimage seems to have made a comeback in the past couple of decades. Picaud's route, the so-called Camino de Santiago, became the first European Cultural Itinerary in 1987, its 709 kilometres from the Pyrenean foothills to Santiago itself clearly marked for foot-weary modern pilgrims whose numbers increase every year. I saw them in clusters by the roadside, or (not infrequently) alone, sunburnt faces turned to the ground and seemingly oblivious to their surroundings. You see, I was travelling in the opposite direction in a comfortable car. Pilgrimage is as much a physical ordeal as a mental state, and I had neither time nor inclination for the former. Not for me the camaraderie of the walker. After talking to several hundred thousand people each morning for a living, I didn't want to converse with anyone. Does this sound peculiar? I wanted to tip out the baggage of an already overloaded mind and make way for ... nothing. Buddhist meditators would call it achieving a state of 'vacuity', the idea being that one can 'see' things more clearly when there's nothing much going on. Some would maintain that I had been audibly vacuous for some time.

Mere anonymity was not enough. I wanted to be irrelevant, so that my normally well-cultivated field of concerns could be narrowed down to things like ... where will I sleep tonight? What to eat, how to ask for it? I thought that it would be quaint to exchange a reasonable loquacity for the verbal prowess of a Spanish infant. Despite all of our customary precautions, one normally feels strange in a strange place. I wanted to draw this feeling of 'foreignness' around me like a thick cloak, one that I could study from the inside even if the outside appearance was one of ineptitude.

Sounds great, I hear you say, Christopher travelled to Europe so he could feel vacuous and look inept. Of course I went for a good time too, especially one that involved rising late. What bliss! Eventually I bumbled amiably on the wrong side of the road for some 4,500 kilometres, keeping remarkably true to my original itinerary — Pau (in France); Cantabria, Asturias and Galicia along the Spanish coast; Santiago itself, nowadays a lively university city, its bands of pipe-playing students mingling with the wind-whipped pilgrim arrivals; Cabo Finisterre, the place where the world ended for the medievals (as the word suggests). After travelling to the end of the earth I turned eastwards again and returned to France, stopping along the way at a couple of monasteries for tea, a bunk, and an eavesdrop on the monks' ritual singalong.

Enough of the broad brush stuff; what about the detail? It's these minutiae that make the experience, after all. I did attend a broadcaster friend's birthday party in Uzès that featured a makeshift jazz band from a wide list of French and English eccentrics. They were there in force on this sunny Languedoc afternoon, spilling their improvisations into an oncoming mistral that eventually carried both music and paper plates like salad-bearing hovercraft into the grounds of the electrical sub-station and local mental asylum directly across the street.

I think it was Byron who stated that 'high mountains are a feeling'. Certainly I was feeling something around the upper thighs as I strode around the Pyrenees for seven days in the company of some Australians, together with a sprinkling of curious locals. The dramatic expenditure of carbohydrates no doubt explained the vigour with which we attacked ducks, rabbits and snails every evening back at our hotel. One afternoon, still glowing from exertion and exhilaration after tackling the monumental Cirque de Gavarnie — a huge curtain of rock on the French/Spanish border — our bus stopped to pick up some hitch-hikers. They were two obviously milk-fed German girls, who explained between fits of giggles that they were also making a pilgrimage to Santiago; their goal being to lose weight. (Good to see Saint James in there competing with Jenny Craig.) Their laughter consumed the rest of the bus; so much so that one of the more senior walkers, visibly stunned by the girls' fleshly opulence, turned moist eyes in my direction and confided, 'Ah, Chris ... you wouldn't be dead for quids.' Such loquacity in these circumstances made this the most profound utterance of the trip.

Things were equally boisterous in a little hill village further east called Aiglun (population 28). Here, by courtesy of an Australian friend, I met and befriended the local builder, Rocco Rossini. Any resemblance to another famous name is based on bloodline; Rocco proudly boasted of his close family ties to the great composer. Certainly he inherited a fondness for the pleasures of the table. All of our conversations took place at the casa Rossini during long lunches and dinners which somehow merged into each other with barely enough pause for Rocco to shoulder a gun and bring back another wild boar from the surrounding hills (strictly in season, of course). So long, Rocco, and thanks for the *sanglier*.

So, the suspenders have slipped, the mind is emptied, and in following the examples of our distinguished musical predecessors we have arrived — where? A state of readiness for the new ... **Hope**.

⇢ HOPE ⇠

"Pleiades: Kungkarungkara ... Sirius: Warepil ...
Crux Australis: Waluwara ..."

ROSS EDWARDS, *Star Chant*, 2001 (text by Fred Watson)

Hope in action: a composer lives on the other side
of my back lane. He spends his time these days
writing music for stars — the ones in the sky.

MOST MORNINGS I cross the lane with my two dogs and go
around the block so that I can stroll past the front of the
house where Ross Edwards lives with his wife, Helen, and
their two grown-up kids (sometimes). He's usually there in
a room overlooking the street, hunched over an electric
piano with an enormous corkboard studded with manuscript sheets propped up before him. If it's a big orchestral
work, like a symphony, the acreage of paper is considerable.
On lucky days he'll ask me in for a chat and a play-through
of the piece in progress.

187

Ross isn't remotely whimsical in his work patterns. He is a dedicated craftsman who picks up tools at the beginning of what we call 'office hours' and continues well after most of us have adjourned to the pub for end-of-day consolation. Pick, pick, pick at the keyboard: scribble, scribble. Rub out. Rewrite. He must run up quite a bill in pencils. All the better for erasure, I suppose, because those crotchets don't just drop onto the paper as if summoned from thin air. A symphony doesn't arrive like fine weather. This, to me, looks like hard work; real labour. Music is something a composer actually *makes*. Ross is obviously a real composer, so all I can conclude is that the rest of them must have worked their butts off as well.

***

A composer lives on the other side of my back lane. How exotic. I might just as well have written that I keep a living dodo in the cellar. One assumes composers to be a rare species indeed — if not actually extinct. How could those periwigged woodland creatures of old have survived in today's world? The chainsaw of economic rationalism has logged their old cultural habitats. Rich people don't keep their own house orchestras busy on a weekly diet of new symphonies any more. The opera-going public isn't clamouring for this month's latest hit. Our society doesn't have the time, or more importantly, the money to support artists who insist on producing something so ... so commercially useless.

Television themes or commercial jingles are the pathways of the labourer composer these days; as for the forest of a symphony or the tundra of music theatre — who wants to go there?

The Australian composer Ross Edwards does. In fact, he's never happier than when he's inside a symphony — or a forest, for that matter. Ross can take the sound of a forest and turn it into a symphony. His music almost seems to have sprouted from the loam in some isolated gully, pulsing with a sonic sap inspired in part by the sound of birds and insects encountered during the composer's walks and meditations in the bush. The natural world even infuses many of his titles: *Mountain Village in a Clearing Mist; Prelude and Dragonfly Dance; Raft Song at Sunrise; White Cockatoo Spirit Dance.*

Birdsong has cropped up in music over the ages, but almost always as quotation. Think of the second movement ending in Beethoven's Sixth Symphony, called the 'Pastoral'. It's like Beethoven standing up during party charades and saying, '… here's my imitation of a bird.' Now there's something to contemplate.

Ross Edwards isn't the charades type. I can't imagine him drawing attention to himself at any party. He doesn't do bush 'impressions'. The listener doesn't sit through an Edwards piece waiting to recognise the grasshopper. No specimens under glass adorn his music's walls. They *are* the walls; sounds from nature re-emerging as musical symbols, bent every which way to create the figurations, contours, rhythms and textures of an ever-expanding body of work.

Ross was born in Sydney in 1943. He has no recollection of a childhood enthusiasm for the heavens. But now that he's lived longer than Beethoven and enjoys an international reputation, Edwards is writing his fourth symphony — commissioned for the 2002 Adelaide Festival — and after a lifetime of singing about the world, he is reaching for the stars via an incantatory choral work with a text by the astronomer Fred Watson, listing major stars and constellations as they spin in sequence through an Australian night sky. Their classical names are juxtaposed with the Aboriginal equivalents; Edwards and Watson are admirers of indigenous cultures. The symphony is called *Star Chant*.

This particular morning Ross has ushered me into his workroom. He isn't a technophile but concessions have been made to the modern world. One benchtop contains a fax machine, a photocopier, scanner and PC for emails and regular inspection of his personal website. Ross navigates these functions with the caution and success rate of a learner driver. (Older composers with a more mathematical bent would doubtless have relished the cyber-world. I'm convinced that Mozart would have made a fortune writing software.)

Still, these are merely the flashing lights in a mystic's cave — or a forest burrow. Ross has a slight 'Wind in the Willows' look about him, despite the tropical shirt. I can see him at the back of Rat's boat shyly sipping another lemonade, or more likely, a riesling. Slight behind a mole-hill of embonpoint, tousle-haired, bearded, a soft candour in his eyes, he looks both youthful and avuncular. Edwards is comfortable in his habitat because it helps him reduce his existence to one purpose. After all, creative artists don't merely toss ideas around in their heads; they often have to bounce them off the walls. This particular room has incubated two symphonies already with a third on the way. Does the music still resonate deep down in these atoms? I remember being in the writing room of Ravel's house outside Paris years before and quietly pressing my ear to an architrave on the off-chance of hearing a faint ripple of the *Bolero*. Ravel, being long dead, was not there to disapprove. He would have lamented my taste in shirts.

Ross is sitting at the piano before his giant corkboard and its tiers of notation. Peering up at the top left corner sheet, he begins to play the opening of his symphony while rendering a Tibetan throat-singer's impression of a choir. I can swear I see stars and check my scalp for any concussion. It is the music itself that has poleaxed me, of course.

It is humbling to be serenaded by a composer with music that no-one else has heard. Surely there is nothing more important going on in the world at this moment. There is an integrity to the work that fills the air between us and seals the music's existence irrespective of the number of its future listeners. It is *there*. We just have to hope that some of us will be lucky enough to find it.

⚜

What is the best thing to hope for in this life? If composers are any guide, it is to discover one's song and learn to sing it. The search can be agonising. For a lucky few, the knowledge is as obvious as stubbing a toe.

Ross Edwards was aware of music in his head as a child. When he was thirteen he was taken to an orchestral concert and heard live music-making at this sophisticated level for the first time. He had stubbed his toe. Two toes, in fact, perhaps spraining his foot, realising at once that there was only one thing he wanted to do, but that he was going to have to work hard to learn how to do it.

Secondary school was no help. Edwards describes his early education as at best 'an inconvenience', at worst 'a concentration camp'. As an only child he was naturally the focus of his parents' highest expectations and it was thought that young Ross might become an architect. Since architecture has been called 'frozen music', the Edwards family wasn't far off the mark, but the budding composer with some talent for drawing had already chosen barlines over balustrades.

This was the late 1950s in Australia and such a career choice was unorthodox. To be a composer now is still considered exotic; back in the time of Menzies, however, such bohemian leanings were simply outlandish. Edwards went through conservatorium and university in Sydney and Adelaide, gaining a Bachelor of Music in 1968 and becoming the star character in a number of musical urban myths that I would love to include here. I had fellow composers Peter Sculthorpe and Vincent Plush recite them for me in a radio documentary I made about Edwards in 1984. Essentially, they are variations on the theme of the absent-minded innocent abroad; the womble caught in the headlight-glare of a crass world. Ross swears they're all false and that my broadcasting them in the first place caused some hurried explanations to his in-laws. I believe him now because the affable woodland creature aura doesn't match with such quiet determination.

Have I made a mistake? By the late 1960s Edwards was in London, later in an isolated farmhouse in Yorkshire, refining the singing of his song. We're told that ease of expression comes with a developing technique, but Edwards began to find the opposite to be the case. Alone with his sheets of manuscript paper, he harboured doubts about the direction of all his work up to that moment. He had trapped himself inside the wrong song.

⸻

The decision that one has been going in the wrong direction in life is one of the most terrifying we can make. It is one that many of us avoid because the consequences would be just too harrowing; what happens to the reputation, the self-esteem — the mortgage? Until quite recently, making such a judgement was considered to be capricious and premature if the persons judging themselves were young; for those who were older it was thought of as a symptom of 'mid-life crisis' (see Chabrier in **Joy**). Go back, you are going the wrong way? Nonsense! Once out of the starting blocks, we were not supposed to deviate from the lane boundaries. Anything that involved self-appraisal, or worse, self-renewal, was a cop-out. Cop-outs are for wimps.

These days there is a refreshing new awareness that a life can encompass several careers. In the case of a creative artist, 'career' is not the point at issue, however; it is something more fundamental, more intimate — a judgement about the very core of their being, the point of their existence. When a shadow falls across a lifetime of previous assumptions about oneself, the results can be cathartic. So it was for Edwards, who admits that at the time he was '… physically sick at the thought of some of the music I'd been writing; just torrents of notes saying the world is awful and here I am in it. It was entirely neurotic stuff. I was fighting against a system that I didn't believe in. I was trying to make something work that never could work. I simply realised you've gotta stop doing this.'

From 1974 to 1976, Ross wrote virtually nothing. By now in his thirties and having already had his works performed around Australia and overseas, it was a potentially dangerous situation to be in when strategy might have dictated a speeding-up of activity. Edwards had decided to take a more intuitive approach to his work. 'At this stage,' he says, 'my instincts told me to stop trying.'

***

Let it go and it will come back: The stillness that must precede renewal will be familiar to those of a contemplative nature. A two-year stillness is a long hiatus in the early part of a working life. But silence is an important element of Edwards' work, and he gradually began to accept this creative silence as a constructive necessity.

'The solution was for me to learn to relinquish a lot of control,' Edwards says. And in creating this space around himself, fresh messages began to arrive — not from the 'awful' world from which he had felt increasingly alienated, but from the natural world; the bush sounds of birds and insects who were the in-house minstrels at Pearl Beach on the New South Wales coast where the composer lived with his young family in the late seventies. His true song was all around him.

***

What emerged from this hibernation were two distinct and contrasting styles. One, called his 'sacred' style, takes us deep into the quiet of the soul, a lush silent darkness flecked sparsely by pinpoints of sound. It feels like heresy to have to dwell in these silences in the company of anyone else, which perhaps explains why Ross is uncomfortable with the listening environment of the concert hall; all those people just bursting to cough. It's like taking the delicate flutterings and scuttlings of his music and nailing it to a wall. Short of transporting busloads of listeners to the nearest national park and serenading them through an invisible sound system, Ross sometimes requests that the lights in the performance space be dimmed.

Anyway, why be inside a concert hall when you can be on top? His *Dawn Mantras*, first performed just before sunrise on New Year's Day 2000 and telecast around the globe, perched a young girl singer, a shakuhachi (bamboo flute), two Burmese gongs and a didjeridu atop the sails of the Sydney Opera House, juxtaposing sounds — and therefore, cultures — in a glorious slow-motion song of hope, arcing as high and wide as the dawning sky above them. For many, it was the highlight of what was otherwise a 24-hour international fireworks display.

The other style is what Ross calls his 'maninya' style. The word sounds vaguely Indonesian to me, but Ross says it is his own invention. Whatever it is, one can't try to pronounce it without inflecting the word with rhythm; likewise, it describes his 'kick yer shoes off and hit the floor' work — lightness, spontaneity, the rush to dance. He has written several pieces with the word as their title; the largest of them being his 1988 Violin Concerto, given the plural *Maninyas*.

Back in my sound producer days I was lucky enough to be entrusted with the studio recording of this work for commercial release with the Sydney Symphony Orchestra, conductor Stuart Challender and soloist Dene Olding. The venture was a success, winning recording awards in Australia and Europe, but whenever I hear it those fond memories of the working experience are elbowed aside and I marvel at the music all over again. The score seems to shine from the inside. It pays a ritual homage to the earth with its emphatic but soft-edged pulsing. We are dancing on moss. Fragments of melody are happily reiterated like kids calling each other to play. The middle movement is the reflective flip side of this exuberance; a modern slow plainchant on the violin over a grave processional intoned by low strings. I once conducted this movement in what was essentially a 'comedy' concert in Tasmania. At the music's conclusion, I turned to the soloist and noticed tears streaming down her face. She wasn't laughing.

<hr />

Retuning: Edwards doesn't write 'religious' music in the Christian, denominational sense of the term. He has quoted from medieval plainsong, most notably the *Ave Maria Gratia Plena* (Hail Mary, full of grace), placing Mary at the centre of a more pantheistic belief; to him, She represents 'the universal and eternal feminine spirit, the Earth Mother, source and nurturer of all living things'. In fact, I have no idea of Ross' faith at all but I suspect any musings on the hereafter are secondary to his concerns for fixing up the here and now. He assigns a function to his work in a dislocated world, saying that, '… it's not only possible — it's essential to write music that can rebalance, harmonise and heal instead of music that describes the world we've just come out of. I know it's naive, but you have to have a certain amount of naivety otherwise you would just go mad.'

⌐⊱⊰⌐

Faith is only a genuflection away from hope. If you believe, then do it with music. That simplistic tenet has been classical music's most prodigious inspiration. There's hardly a composer in this book who didn't have a crack at a liturgical piece. Many of the masses, motets and processionals that resulted are so beautiful we don't have to go to church to hear them. Mind you, the Church was protective of its musical treasures. The famous setting of the *Miserere* by **Gregorio Allegri** (1582–1652) was kept a secret by the papal choir (for whom it was composed) in the Sistine Chapel for hundreds of years; nary a trickle of its polyphony was allowed to escape those Michelangelo-encrusted walls, either in sound or on paper. When the fourteen-year-old Mozart wrote the whole thing out from memory after a single hearing in 1770, he risked excommunication; instead, the amazed Pope Clement XIV awarded him the Order of the Golden Spur. (Mozart later discovered his miraculous transcription contained several mistakes.) **Johann**

Sebastian Bach (1685–1750) is something close to God for many musicians. He would have been horrified by the comparison, since for him writing music was a way of sending emails upstairs. The overwhelming bulk of his output was composed for liturgical purposes (he was a cantor) and frequently dedicated 'to the Glory of God'.

Composers also exercised their faith through ordination. Becoming a priest in those days was not only a matter of receiving God's summons; it was also a solid career option. **Antonio Vivaldi** (1678–1741) was known as the 'Red Priest' of Venice on account of his hair colour. Some say he was an asthmatic and was excused from saying Mass because his wheezing diluted the power of the Word. He was also prone to leaving the altar mid-sentence if an idea for a fugue suddenly struck him. There was no time to waste when it came to composing; his young charges at the Pio Ospedale della Pietà (a home for orphaned or abandoned girls) needed a steady diet of new concertos for their musical education. They must have been pretty good; Vivaldi turned out more than five hundred in his lifetime (concertos, that is).

Despite the obvious benefits of his teaching Vivaldi was voted in and out of his job several times by the institution's governors and in 1737 was censured for conduct unbecoming to a priest. In some respects the carrot-topped man of God was all too worldly, it appears. He maintained an entourage on his too-frequent travels that included two sisters; one a former singing pupil, the other his 'nurse'. Tongues wagged.

Vivaldi was also a hard and shrewd businessman when it

came to doing publishing deals and the dozen collections of his concertos published during his lifetime earned him some very comfortable amounts of cash which he just as quickly spent (on his entourage, presumably). There was certainly nothing left when he expired in the house of a Viennese saddler's widow, his pockets and his reputation in tatters. The wizard of the violin and creator of the *Four Seasons* (1725), the baroque era's biggest contribution to modern restaurant music, was hustled quickly into a pauper's grave.

More devout was one of my favourite monks, the Spaniard **Antonio Soler** (1729–1783) who composed furiously within the quiet confines of his cloister. His *Fandango* for harpsichord is one of the daffiest keyboard pieces of the eighteenth century, oscillating hypnotically between two chords for all its 450 bars.

Interesting near-priests include **Domenico Zipoli** (1688–1726), who went off to South America from his native Italy to be a Jesuit missionary (rather like in the film *The Mission*) but expired in Argentina with tuberculosis before receiving his final orders. An arrangement of one of his adagios into a piece called *Elevazione* was one of the most popular works I ever played on the radio — it's in one of the *Swoon* collections on CD.

Giuseppe Tartini (1692–1770) would doubtless have completed his studies for the priesthood had it not been for his skill as a swordsman, his illicit marriage at the age of eighteen, and the fathering of an illegitimate son with his Venetian landlady. Legend has it that the theme of

Tartini's most famous violin sonata was played to him in a dream by the Devil — it is called the *Devil's Trill*.

Franz Liszt took minor orders in the Catholic Church in 1865 after a series of personal tragedies, including the early deaths of two of his children, and his longtime mistress' repeatedly unsuccessful attempts to be granted a divorce from her first husband, thereby paralysing their own wedding plans. The despondent pianist/composer was given a suite of rooms by a cardinal in Rome's Villa d'Este, where the once restless sybarite occupied himself by writing religious music. You must try and have a listen to Liszt's rarely-performed or recorded oratorio *Christus* written with a spareness and simplicity worlds away from the thick cascades of his virtuoso keyboard music.

Liszt's son-in-law **Richard Wagner** came to believe that music and art could take over when religion lost its potency. The three came together in Wagner's valedictory *Parsifal* (1882), described as a 'sacred stage festival play' by the composer, who further emphasised the sense of ritual in performance by banning audience applause between the first and second acts. The story revolves around the Holy Grail, Parsifal himself is a Christ-like figure, and 'Faith' even receives its own melodic motif. That Wagner died six months after its premiere should come as no surprise; the chorus that crowns the work sounds like a transport to heaven. When the dancing stops at my own wake I wouldn't mind the end of *Parsifal* played as a musical chaser. It is sublime.

Music is always there when even the most corrupt and despicable cast their eyes heavenward. The courtesan Thaïs finds God one night to the strains of a solo violin in the 1894 performance of the opera *Thaïs* by **Jules Massenet** (1842–1912). In this, the opera's most famous moment, no voice will do; but the beautiful *Meditation* failed to convince a cool audience at the Paris Opéra premiere. Deciding that the evening needed a little spicing up, the lead soprano Sybil Sanderson 'accidentally' flashed her Californian bust, much to the delight of the infatuated composer. Her breasts were apparently the only things about the opera that the critics remembered.

Faith … or lack thereof: Towards the end of his life, in the closing chapter of his *Mémoires*, Berlioz described music as one of 'the wings of the soul' (see **Love with Violins**). The agnostic composer couldn't be as sure of the soul's destination. The dramatist in Berlioz seized upon the *Dies Irae* section of his 1837 setting of the Requiem Mass with relish in one of music's great cataclysms (as one would expect for the end of the world), but the spiritual elements of the text find no similar fulfilment. There is no reassurance about life's mystery, no attempted explanation; the only certainty is that of the grave. One of the most extraordinary moments occurs in the *Hostias* — only forty-seven bars long, intoned as a chordal chant by the men in the chorus accompanied by low trombones and high flutes. The effect is of whispering harmonics over a pedal note — but it is also more unsettling, even sinister than that. Berlioz does not permit us the beatific certitude of a Bach or triumphant resolve of a Beethoven. Years later, he would quote from Shakespeare's *Macbeth* at the head of his own *Mémoires*: 'Life's but a walking shadow …', but already in the emptiness of the *Hostias* he is making us peer into the void.

❦

Early evening: My wife and I made arrangements today to scuttle across the back lane to the Edwards' for drinks and stir-fry. Helen Edwards has just rung: Ross is having a productive day with the Fourth Symphony. Could we delay the start of dinner for a short while? He is 'bringing in the horns'. I suspect that I'll never be able to hear the Symphony in future without feeling hungry.

❦

When hope is gone: A famous example of music's restorative powers occurred in 1737 when King Philip V of Spain was suffering from such a long-term depression that he was neglecting affairs of state. He'd even stopped shaving. After numerous futile attempts to lift his spirits, his wife arranged for the famous Italian castrato Farinelli to knock out a couple of numbers in the royal apartments. The music and the beauty of the singer's surgically preserved soprano did the trick; the King's stubble was quickly removed. Farinelli's musical cure became instantly addictive — he had to serenade the King with the same four songs every night for the next twenty years.

⌐≈≈≈⌐

A return of royal good spirits is proof of music's capacity to heal. Ross Edwards believes that society today has inherited plenty of cracks, between 'matter and spirit, masculine and feminine, mind and body and so on' (he writes this about his Third Symphony). He also has a hope — better than this, a belief — that we increasingly feel the need for balance and conciliation, which he expresses by 'trying quite consciously to write beautiful music, whereas a few years ago you would have been ostracised for it'.

Ross should know. Much of his work in recent years has met a frosty reception from some fellow composers and the odd critic. Edwards' idea of 'beauty' in music finds an accord with many audiences around the world and this

204

implicit ease of access raises the hackles of some hardheads in the 'serious' music world (many of whose works are played less often, I suspect). According to this lofty fraternity, if the typical concert-goer appears to like a new piece too readily it must be assumed that he or she hasn't had to work too hard to find their way into it; ergo, the composer has 'written down' to them. I must say this constant assumption of the public's 'stupidity' irritates me. Having been privileged to talk to the public for many years in the course of broadcasting, I've learned to admire and respect the sincerity of its response to music that might induce a sneer from some. If you or I are immediately moved by a piece, be it new or old, we don't want that very personal experience invalidated by an accusation that we weren't listening properly, or that the piece must have been too 'easy'. *Really*.

But it has always been like this. Composers love having a go at each other, and they are certainly good at it. Musical invective over the ages makes great reading, even when it is misplaced. Tchaikovsky called Brahms a 'giftless bastard'.

<hr />

At the end of Stanley Kubrick's film *2001: A Space Odyssey*, a Star-Child still in embryo floats out of the cosmos and casts a benign gaze over the earth. Is it God? Has the aged ex-astronaut from which its cosmic placenta magically sprung been eating some strange brownies? Whatever it means, the image suggests hope and regeneration. I don't know if this enigmatic visitor will finally be named in Ross Edwards' *Star Chant*. It does feel good, though, when creative artists finally decide to join scientists in returning the imagined stare from out there.

⸻

Our guide now draws up to the long final chord and a destination even beyond the stars. Even hope can be covetous when it is entertained rashly. It is time to leave our emotions behind us.

⇥ PEACE ⇤

"Music exists to elevate us as far as possible above everyday experience."
GABRIEL FAURÉ, 1908

We come to our final blissful chapter like a weary traveller at the end of the journey, having been whipped raw by the succession of emotional extremes displayed by our noble crew of fools for love. Time for rest; time to *Swoon*. In medical parlance, a swoon is a syncope — a faint. The sight of blood, the sound of the Beatles, the tossing of a lock of hair by Franz Liszt; all could induce this loss of consciousness. Listening must be difficult when all the lights are out upstairs. But 'Swooning' to classical music came to mean something else for thousands of Australians who tuned in to the radio each morning or purchased the CDs with the title. It was an invitation to enter a passageway to a different — perhaps a higher — consciousness; a pleasure so profound that it transcended mere indulgence. It offered … Peace.

WE COME ALMOST to the point where words will simply not do. I was tempted to take a Zen approach here and include several blank pages culminating with 'The End' in very small print on the back fly leaf. It would have allowed you space to record your own reactions to music that takes you to a special place. Rather, I shall share with you some of mine. But first, an introduction to the Ultimate Peace Tour Guide …

> *"Thus am I … a small feather from the ground*
> *commanded to fly …"*
> HILDEGARD OF BINGEN (1098–1179)

… a beautiful image. And the Abbess Hildegard was full of them. They came to her as visions which she eventually wrote down in a book called *Scivias*, or 'Know the Ways'. I called her a guide, and so she was: a guide, a confidante, an advisor, a diplomat and a correspondent for popes, kings and emperors around medieval Europe. They wanted to know the ways in practical and spiritual matters, and the woman known as the 'Sybil of the Rhine' appeared to be getting the answers from an impeccable source. 'It is said that you are raised to Heaven, that much is revealed to you, and that you bring forth great writings and discover new manners of song …', wrote one Master Odo of Paris in an 1148 fan letter. In fact, her fan club was enormous; Hildegard of Bingen was the most famous and influential woman of her time.

Another millennium has rolled by since then and we are singing her songs more than ever. Is this because we are

newly inspired by their devotional content? Not entirely —
although we live at a time when the frantic pursuit of mat-
erialism is losing some of its glamour, and there is plenty of
devotional music in various liturgies that fails to match the
exalted sentiments contained within their texts. No — we
sing the music of Hildegard because it is some of the greatest
music ever written. If her messages were indeed of divine
origin one can only say that she had a good connection.

How to 'get' peace? How many books about this do you
want to read? I've read a few, because arriving at the state
of experiencing life that Hildegard managed to sustain
seems to me one of the best things we can do for ourselves.
The effort of trying to get there is what counts, and the
techniques are as wide-ranging as the gap between East and
West, as numerous as the religions, cults, gurus and meditation retreats that proliferate around the world. Hildegard
operates within the Christian tradition, and the magnificent
poetry with which she expresses her visions abounds in
Christian symbolism: old and new 'wine' can represent the
Testaments; Mary can be 'the greenest branch'; God's love
the 'heat of the sun' blazing in a dark sanctuary; Christ's love
a 'latticed window'; The Holy Ghost, a dove. They are
beautiful, lush, richly coloured images.

And they're in Latin, of course. Understanding the text
is essential as a devotional aid if Christian worship is your

way 'up'. But if all Latin is Greek to you, or you simply cannot read the poetry while your eyes are closed in meditation, Hildegard's music is a marvellous vehicle in itself. She gathered her melodies in the *Symphonia armonie celestium revalationum* (Symphony of the Harmony of Celestial Revelations). They are pure melody — unaccompanied, unadorned, a single strand of sound that embodies all thought and encloses the whole spirit and body as it is produced. At least, that is the ideal. It is not just a song; it is a device for meditation, called plainchant. The music is meant to be used, rather than overheard. That is why I become tetchy when it is served up as an accompaniment to dinner parties these days. (I'm actually pretty relaxed about classical 'muzak', believing that most composers would be delighted with the royalties if they were still alive. Schubert won't be harmed by having his Unfinished Symphony heard in a lift.)

Hildegard was the tenth child of a German noble family. As such, she was promised to the Church and by the age of eight was packed off to begin her noviciate with a nearby recluse, Jutta of Spanheim, who lived in a cell. Eight! That was the extent of medieval vocational guidance. Fortunately, she took to the contemplative life like a duck to water — she might have said like a dove to lattice — and one could ponder whether her achievement would have been anywhere near as considerable if she'd simply been married off to some princeling down the road.

⟨~≈⊱⊰≈~⟩

Clarity of vision: Hildegard took the veil at fifteen and became the Abbess of Jutta's order of nuns upon the latter's death in 1136. Five years later, now entering middle age — a reasonable span already in the Middle Ages, when middle age was about fifteen — she saw flames descend upon her from Heaven. She felt (understandably) she should get a move on. Thereafter Hildegard founded her own monastery in the Rhine valley near Bingen with eighteen other sisters and devoted herself to creativity, writing down her visions plus poetry, music, hagiography and treatises on natural history and medicine. This breadth of vision is hard to reconcile with a woman who had spent her life up to this point in a cell saying nothing much to a recluse. These days people spend their lives in a small room saying nothing at all to a television set but fail to develop similar intellectual interests.

After Hildegard's death in 1179 four popes initiated processes that would have led to her canonisation. The last was John XXII (1316–34) but things have slowed since then; probably at the wrong end of an in-tray. Hildegard does have a feast day, though; give her a peaceful thought on 17 September.

There was nothing remotely sinister about Hildegard's visions, apparently — no twisting or foaming on the floor, no eyes rolling back in the head at midnight. It was a peaceful process, almost like the miraculous imposition of an alternate reality around her. What were they putting in the tea at Rupertsberg?

Peaceful recollections

Live and learn: Piano Quintet No.2: 1st movement (Fauré). The older I become the more this strikes me as one of the greatest pieces ever written. **Gabriel Fauré** lived a good long span — he was born in 1845 and died in 1924, composing right through to the end. The Second Quintet is one of the very last things he wrote and to my ears every minute of his life experience is inside it. Or is it every minute of *my* life experience? If music is something like an X-ray mirror with those innermost parts of ourselves bouncing out of the sound, then we all face the delightful prospect of coming to appreciate and understand great music purely because our self-knowledge has increased. Music is one of the great barometers of our progress and growth through life. It can be forever associated with watershed moments in our personal existence like aural souvenirs, but it also lets us know when we're ready to move on to the next destination in the big spiritual tour. The composers — our guides — have often been there before. But theirs is not an exceptional journey; or rather, it's as exceptional as the one we all experience.

Artists teach us nothing; they simply point out the things we did not know we actually knew. I never expect 'wisdom' from classical music. If anything, I relish the confirmation that most of the composers were as ill-informed and 'un-lived' as I feel. A year before the premiere of his complete *Ring* cycle in 1876, the sixty-two-year-old Richard Wagner is alleged to have said, '… I know nothing at all about music.' Mind you, I would kill to be as ignorant as Wagner. Unfortunately no-one can discover the real limits of their knowledge overnight; it takes a lifetime of crashing into reality's walls.

Well, this Second Piano Quintet by Fauré sounds to me as if he has collected the memories of his many collisions, accepted their necessity, and then let them go. The music doesn't look heavenward as in his much earlier *Requiem*, in which the serenity feels a little drugged; death is a matter of going to sleep. The Quintet is more truly valedictory; after all, the composer was in his mid-seventies when he wrote it. I remember its use in a 1984 film called *A Sunday in the Country*, directed by Bertrand Tavernier. An aged artist sits in his *atelier* as the sun sets on a day of family drama. Widowed and alone, aware of his declining powers and the limit of his talent, he peers through the dusk at an incomplete still-life on his easel … then at the liver spots on his wrinkled hands. The camera quietly cuts away from the artist's contemplation and drifts slowly to the view over his lush garden from an open window. At the end of the day, at the end of the struggle, all that remains — if we are well-intentioned, diligent and lucky — is a little piece of beauty.

Fauré's music says this to me as it flows through this last wordless scene. It is always a privilege to taste the fruit of a life that has been fully resolved through living. On his deathbed, three years after the Second Quintet's premiere, Fauré said, '… I did what I could.'

Deep peace: A traditional Gaelic blessing, given the simplest of settings by American composer Bill Douglas and one of the most popular pieces I ever played on-air:

Deep peace of the running wave to you
Deep peace of the flowing air to you
Deep peace of the quiet earth to you
Deep peace of the shining stars to you
Deep peace of the gentle night to you
Moon and stars pour out their healing light to you
Deep peace to you.

Christmas Concerto, Op.6, No.8: *Pastorale* (Corelli). As a professional gossip I'm always on hand to offer unsolicited advice. Being asked to provide guidance is a more terrifying responsibility. So when people new to classical music call or write to me with that question 'Where do I start?', I almost never know what to say. One person's Brahms is another's offal (actually, I think Brahms was partial to offal). For Tchaikovsky, Brahms *was* offal (see **Hope**). Tchaikovsky and Brahms wrote a violin concerto apiece. Both are master-pieces. If forced to choose between them, however, I'd plump for the Brahms in which the cantankerous habitué of Viennese pastry shops allows us a good look under the crust. Forget the crust; I simply prefer Brahms' music in this concerto form and have done ever since I was a teenager. Tchaikovsky would have written me off for this, I suspect.

Brahms may well be too rich an ambrosia for some with a virginal musical palate. A few paprika-laden sips of his Hungarian Dances may help here.

The baroque era is often cited as being the place for neophytes; all that 'clarity' of texture and driving rhythm supposedly bearing some affinity with much of the popular music of today. This may well be the case, although I recall as a ten-year-old submitting my Beatles-drenched ears to Bach's first couple of Brandenburg Concertos and having no idea of what was going on. I'd been brought up on 'vertical' music — a single (and frequently wonderful) tune running along like electrical cable atop solid harmonic poles. On the other hand, Bach's music was entirely 'horizontal', containing several different melodies all going at the same time, like simultaneous babble from six people at the next table in a foreign restaurant. The ear soon learns to delight in such combinations.

Putting these doubts aside, I always recommend the Opus 6 collection of *concerti grossi* (an early form of the concerto) by the Italian master violinist **Corelli** (1653–1713). He's an obvious candidate for inclusion in this chapter on the sole basis of his first name, which was Arcangelo, or 'Archangel'. What a brilliant opening line that would have been at a Roman party in the 1670s … 'Hi there, gorgeous, guess my name and I'll take you to Heaven.' Actually, he was named after his father, who had died (and had presumably joined that celestial rank) a month before the composer's birth. Corelli had a serene countenance until he picked up his violin, when all facial hell would break loose with red eyeballs rolling '… as if in an agony'. His diabolical performance manner was contrasted by his compositions which an eighteenth-century writer described as 'chaste'. Chastity is probably a useful quality to bring to a musical evocation of Christ's birth in this concerto from his posthumously published set of Opus 6 (Corelli was possibly the least prolific of the really great composers).

The *Pastorale* which concludes the work seems like a rustic shepherd's song over a droning accompaniment; a stained-glass version of what eighteenth-century folk music was like. Corelli may have been inspired by the music of the Abruzzi shepherds outside of Rome who would come into town to celebrate the Christmas festival, but it's more likely he was just being fashionable, writing in a genre that celebrated the apparent purity and simplicity of rural life. (Shepherds are usually like this in classical music — see **Joy**.) Fashion is always badmouthed by unsuccessful artists although its origins seem quite reasonable to me — the repetition *ad nauseam* of a publicly-endorsed idea. Since Corelli was both successful *and* wealthy in his career, fashion was just another convenient conduit to public acceptance. When you're as good as he was, the talent shines through anyway.

I may be just a twenty-first-century sentimentalist when I say that the *Pastorale* captures the stillness and magic of that first Christmas Eve in the ancient world. A more cautious compliment then — the music catches the moment and place as we would like them to have been.

The Enchanted Lake (1909). One of the most peaceful of fantasies is that of solitude in a place removed from the importuning 'real' world. Some go to retreats; here is such a musical place. **Anatoly Lyadov** (1855–1914) was perhaps the laziest composer of all; for him to have finished this short work at all represents a major commitment. In fact he makes it twice as long as it could have been by repeating each of its ideas like an incantatory echo.

⸎

Beam me up, Virila: Some advice — if you're looking for peace, a monastery is hard to beat. Hildegard would agree. In modern Spain one doesn't need to beg for refuge from uncomprehending monks; no, several monasteries have hotel annexes with actual reception desks and credit card facilities where rooms can be had at comparatively modest prices. Spartan they may be but, when at their home, do as the monks do. I stayed in two of these Spanish Heavenly Hotels, both in isolated spots — Valvanere, a twelfth-century building in the verdant foothills of the Sierra de la Demanda midway between the cities of Burgos and Logrono; and in Leyre, an even older building further to the north-east of Spain in the very American Wild West-looking area of Navarre. It's said of the latter that one of its eighth-century bishops, one San Virila, constantly prayed for a glimpse of infinity and was granted his wish by a sleep-inducing birdcall that nodded him off for three hundred years.

The monastery has been occupied and run by the Benedictines only since 1950 and they are renowned in Spain for the quality of their plainchant singing. I know this because the winsome reception clerk told me as I checked in. Better still, evensong was starting in five minutes! Off I rushed to the grand but gloomy church above its pre-Romanesque crypt, my arrival boosting the all-tourist congregation to about five. As the clock struck overhead, I was suddenly plunged back into the Middle Ages. Thirty monks dutifully shuffled into the chancel, lighting candles en route, lined up in opposing rows, and sang a complete service heavenward in the flickering light. The sincerity in their singing was so moving that I paid no attention to its technical quality. My recollection is that it was pretty good. More than that, it was the moment when in a strange place I didn't feel strange at all. Peaceful, perhaps.

❦

Ah, Hildegard. What a combination: on the one hand an extraordinary focus of creative energy, an intellectual force bursting through the walls of a medieval monastery, rushing down the Rhine and sweeping up admirers in the courts and cloisters of Europe; on the other, a life given to devotion and a prescribed passivity in her self-description as a mere feather drifting on God's breath. There is wisdom in words spoken softly, and then only rarely. Hildegard never knew the clamour and bustle of secular life, the desperate aspirations of commerce, or sexual love, designer fashion, international travel. She would have disciplined herself to resist most of the emotions we have explored in this book, excepting, of course, Love and a quiet Joy. These are subsumed into her poetry and song, and it's because her music is such an irreducible essence of sound that we feel it embodies some ultimate, necessary Truth. What the Truth is — well, that's up to you. Hildegard of Bingen obviously has a few suggestions, but remember, one person's 'vision thing' is another's donkey vote.

Deep Peace to you.

⤖ CODA ⤖

"The song is ended but the melody lingers on ..."
IRVING BERLIN, *Ziegfield Follies*, 1927

When a concert or recital is over it's customary to
retire to the bar for a drink. When a love affair is
over it's common to take to drink. Some conversation is also involved, although the latter circumstance invites more of a monologue. This is because
we feel that our follies are unique.

THEREFORE I HOPE you take heart from some of the follies
documented here. Our path through life is certainly all ours
but if you listen carefully you can hear the snapping of
branches and cursing of nearby walking disasters. The
woods are alive. What a joy, then, that some of them halted
their blind progress now and then to sing us a song.

We are destined to repeat our follies ad infinitum because
we are human. Soon it will be time to turn back these pages

to the start for more counsel — it's about as close to *Finnegans Wake* as I'll get, that loop of emotion running like a river.

Keep this by the bed for late night reference by all means, but let me conclude (as do many pieces of music in 'sonata' form) with a restatement of the first subject. Now that you've tarried a little on this brackish, pot-holed shoreline, have a little splash in the grand oceanic Real Thing. Listening to some of the music that I've alluded to herein will prove those maxims about the futility of trying to write about it. If this indulgent roam through the lives of some musicians at least suggests the humanity and generosity at the bottom of their collected creative impulse, I'll be delighted. Tackling Beethoven's Fifth will still be your own journey, but you'll never look at his portraits the same way again.

References

Bird, John, *Percy Grainger* (London: Elek Books, 1976).

Cook, Nicholas, *Music: A very short introduction* (Oxford University Press, 1998).

Crofton, Ian and Fraser, David (eds.), *A Dictionary of Musical Quotations* (London: Croom Helm, 1985).

Lebrecht, Norman, *When the Music Stops: Mangers, maestros and the corporate murder of classical music* (London: Simon & Schuster, 1996).

Mémoires de Hector Berlioz (Paris, 1870), quoted in David Cairns, *The Making of an Artist* (Andre Deutsch, 1989).

Mordden, Ethan, *Opera Anecdotes* (New York: Oxford University Press, 1985).

Sadie, Stanley (ed.), *The New Grove Dictionary of Music and Musicians* (London: Macmillan, 1980).